PHR/SPHR Study Guide Bundle! 2 Books In 1! Complete Review & Practice Questions!

By Matt Webber

PHR/SPHR Study Guide – Practice Questions!

Best PHR Test Prep to Help You Prepare for the PHR Exam! Get PHR Certification!

Table Of Contents

Conclusion

Introduction

The PHR Certification Exam is required in order to get an SPHR or PHR certificate. The test is 225 multiple-choice questions, and they have to be answered within four hours. The questions are randomly generated, and each test is unique. In order to pass the test, a score of 500 out of 700 is required.

In addition to passing the exam, you must also have one of the following to receive certification:

- 4 years professional experience in an HR position + a high school diploma

- 2 years professional experience in an HR position + a bachelor's degree

- 1-year professional experience in an HR position + a mas1.ter's degree or higher.

This practice test will help give an idea of the questions that will be on the test, though it is not quite as long. In addition to practice questions, there will also be answers provided, along with an explanation that gives a good understanding of what makes the answer correct. These explanations are also concepts that are seen in the associated study guide, so pairing both together is the best way of preparing for the real test.

These questions are not taken directly from the current test. They have been created based on previous real-test questions, with updated information included. They are different from any other questions you might see, though the basic concepts are the same. If you are not sure of a question, don't panic to answer. Be sure to listen to the explanation that follows. Even if you answer correctly you should still listen to the explanation, as it will help give you reminders and insights on what to expect on the day of the actual test. This information is also included in the study guide, so looking over that beforehand will be sure to help you ace the test.

The most important thing to remember when taking this test, especially more than once, is not to memorize the information. Knowing these answers isn't going to guarantee that you pass the test on the day of the actual examination. These questions only give an idea of the test structure and content.

Each question will have four options, and sometimes more than one of them is the best option. If this is the case, there will be an option for you to choose multiple options. For example, it might be structured as so:

1. Question?

    a. Correct answer

    b. Wrong answer

    c. Correct answer

    d. Both A and C

If this is the case, you are expected to select D as the right answer. Selecting just A or C is incorrect. This means that when you are answering each and every question, you can be sure that there is only one true selection that is correct.

Some questions might involve identifying the different definitions that are used for a specified word or phrase. There might also be a question in which a word is defined, and you are supposed to choose the correct word to go along with this definition. The options might include two words that are very similar, so it's important to make sure that the best option is selected. If something is confusing, try taking a break and going back to it in order to approach the decision with a clearer head.

If at any time you don't understand a question, it might be intentionally structured in a confusing way. In order to make sure that you're not getting caught up on anything small or specific, make sure that you are evaluating each question, and not giving too much time to one that might be intentionally tricky.

This is only a practice exam and does not guarantee any certification. With that being said, it is still a comprehensive test that will give a good idea of what is to be expected. You are encouraged to pair it with other study materials and to take the test more than once, keeping within the time limit of the actual exam. Answering questions in a timely manner will leave you better prepared for when the day comes to take the actual test.

Good luck!

Part 1 – Business Management and Strategy

Business Management and Strategy is an important part of the test. For a list of everything that might be included here, refer to the study guide. There are 18 questions in this part, split between three sections. Though this part is specifically meant to showcase business management and strategy questions, the same core concepts and ideas might be seen throughout different sections of this practice test as well.

Strategic Management

Strategic Management is the first section. This includes anything that might be involved with how an HRM goes about their management strategy.

1. What is included in a job characteristics model?

A. Skill variety

B. Task significance

C. Autonomy

D. All of the above

Answer - D - Skill variety, task significance, and autonomy are all included in a job characteristics model. Not all are required, but they all qualify as answers to the question.

> **Explanation and key takeaway:** A job characteristics model is comprised of five core job characteristics. These are skill variety, task significance, task identity, autonomy, and feedback. From these five characteristics, there are five work-related outcomes that could be a result of this model as well. These are motivation, performance, absenteeism, satisfaction, and turnover. The job characteristics model is a representation of the job characteristics theory. This model has been modified, though the core values are what remains important to an HR manager.

2. Which is NOT included in the strategic role of HR Management?

   A. Planning

B. Discovering organizational objectives

C. Determining employee resistance to a geographical location

D. Issuing polygraph tests to all employees

Answer - D - In terms of the strategic role of HR management, issuing polygraph tests to all employees would not be included. An HRM would, however, plan, discover organizational objectives, and determine an employee's resistance to a geographical location.

> **Explanation and key takeaway:** There are many strategic roles that an HRM has, but polygraph testing is not one of them. This can be remembered by looking at the core administrative functions of an HRM. These are ① training and development, ② benefits administration, ③ recruitment, ④ compensation analysis, and ⑤ general employee administration. Recruitment involves putting the word out there about the job, and initial interviews and background checks. After that, compensation is decided for an individual employee. Employee benefits are considered at this stage as well. Once that

has all been settled, the HRM will guide an employee through their training and development, and later maintain general employee administration. None of these steps would include giving an employee a polygraph test. As an HRM, you won't be expected to give a polygraph test.

3. When making relocation plans, it is important for an HRM analyzing geographic and competitive concerns to first consider:

   A. Foot traffic of a location

   B. An employee's willingness to relocate

   C. Work-family balance

   D. Organizational restructuring

Answer - B - If someone in a managerial position is analyzing geographic and competitive concerns, they must consider a particular employee's willingness to relocate to certain geographical locations. Organizational restructuring might be considered, but only after the employee's willingness to relocate is determined. Foot traffic and work-family balance don't affect what an HR manager might decide.

Explanation and key takeaway: Not every company offers the opportunity of relocation, but when it is presented, the HRM needs to ensure that there is a proper program in place. A relocation scenario would involve a relocation package that presents the benefits of relocation to an eligible employee. As an HR manager, the better prepared you are for relocation services, the smoother everything will go over in this sometimes-challenging position. An HRM has to be aware of all the possibilities, benefits, and risks that are involved in a potential relocation. Relocation should also not be confused with travel opportunities for employees.

4. What kinds of goals are the HRM responsible for?

    A. Individual

    B. Supervisory

    C. Organizational

    D. A and C

Answer - D – The HRM is responsible for individual and organizational goals.

Explanation and key takeaway: There

are many goals that an HRM has, but they are generally individual and organizational. The HRM is responsible for ensuring that an organization reaches its goals, while also making sure that the individual needs of the employees are met. The HRM is responsible for making sure that organizational human resources are being fulfilled, while also ensuring that there is attention given to individual employee needs and issues. An HRM isn't responsible for supervisory goals.

5. When looking to the future, an HR manager can expect that they will have to deal with:

    A. An older workforce

    B. An abundance of entry-level workers

    C. A less radically diverse workforce

    D. Workers that lack skills

Answer - A - As an HR manager looks to the future, they can expect to have to deal with an older workforce. This is especially true for positions that are long-term. As time goes on, the workforce will always become more diverse. Also, an HRM will regularly have to deal with entry-level workers and workers that lack skills throughout their career.

Explanation and key takeaway: The world is changing every single day, but that doesn't mean that an HRM has to constantly and radically change their approach. There are certain trends that are going to stay the same, and that includes dealing with workers that lack skills as well as some entry-level workers. However, as the original workforce becomes older, an HRM will have to develop strategies for dealing with more long-term and seasoned employees.

6. Forecasting involves:

     A. An analysis of a job, an understanding of external conditions, and labor supply projection

     B. An analysis of a job, staffing requirements projection, and labor supply projection

     C. Labor supply projection, staffing requirements projection, and an understanding of external conditions

D. None of the above

Answer - C - Forecasting involves figuring out labor supply projection, staffing requirements projection, and an understanding of external conditions. Forecasting does not include an analysis of a job.

Explanation and key takeaway: At its core, forecasting is when labor needs are projected and predicted, and are used to analyze the effects that might have on a business. Once this basic idea has been discovered, it is then up to the HRM to staff in order to properly ensure that the labor needs are being met.

But the HRM does more than just hire. They also have to ensure that they are taking care of the needs of their current employees, while simultaneously looking at how the new hiring will affect the current status of work. The HRM also needs to check up on how this labor cost is going to affect other parts of the business, such as sales, office space, and the money needed for different benefits, compensations, and insurances. Forecasting is like looking at the weather forecast, only for an HRM, the storm is new hires.

Organizations

This section is going to go over strategic management in terms of how it correlates with different operations. This is not necessarily the order that the test will be in, though it might give the same amount of emphasis to each different subject.

1. Which of the following is NOT one of the four stages of a business lifecycle?

    A. Growth

    B. Maturity

    C. Job design

    D. Rebirth

Answer - C - Job design is not one of the four stages of a business lifecycle. Growth, maturity, and rebirth are three out of the four stages of a business lifecycle.

> **Explanation and key takeaway:** Most businesses go through four stages that affect how they will operate. The first is growth. Whether this is done overnight or over a decade, all businesses go through a period of growth. In this stage, an HRM

would be responsible for overseeing hiring, recruitment, and evaluation of different employees. Job design would be a part of growth, but it would not be its own business lifecycle stage.

As a company goes through the second stage, maturity, the HRM will help in maintaining employee needs, ensuring that different aspects of compensation are being taken care of. This might also include promotion of a business.

The third stage, one that not all businesses will meet, is rebirth. This is when the company gets a new face, whether it's from rebranding, relocating, or recruiting a new managerial staff. The HRM in this process will be responsible for looking back on the company and evaluating what needs to be done to make sure it runs more efficiently.

The final stage is decline, and in this stage, if it happens, the HRM would be responsible for cutting employees and other costs that would help keep the business alive for as long as possible.

2. Forecasting HR demands can be done by using this mathematical method:

A. Productivity ratios

B. Statistical regression analysis

C. Simulation models

D. Any of these would be used

Answer - D - Forecasting HR demands can be done with productivity ratios, statistical regression analysis, or simulation models. Any of these mathematical methods would aid in forecasting, and an HRM is also not limited to these three methods.

> **Explanation and key takeaway:** There are many different methods that an HRM can use to forecast their individual business. For the most part, they would start with setting a goal of what needs to be predicted: Is the HRM looking at an estimation of market demand, or trying to resolve employee turnover? A productivity ratio would assess the number of employees it takes to get a certain task done. This would be helpful in determining how many employees would need to be hired, or which employees could be moved from what departments.
>
> Each of these mathematical methods has a purpose when it comes to forecasting, and

it is up to the HRM to make sure that they are using the best method for the prediction they need. The more aware an HRM is of all the mathematical methods there are to aid in forecasting, the better they will be able to make predictions for their company.

3. Different cultures seek to deal with the fact that the future cannot be perfectly predicted. According to Hofstede's cultural dimensions theory, how can different cultures deal with this?

   A. Power distance

   B. Uncertainty avoidance

   C. Masculinity/femininity

   D. Individualism

Answer - B – Different cultures can deal with the fact that the future cannot be perfectly predicted by using uncertainty avoidance, which is outlined in Hofstede's cultural dimensions theory.

Explanation and key takeaway: According to Hofstede's cultural dimensions theory, uncertainty avoidance is how a society is able to tolerate all of the uncertainty that comes along with day-to-day operations. You can never predict if there's going to be a hurricane that wipes out a planet, or a manager that needs to take sick leave for a month at a time. We might be able to make certain predictions based on guesses, but there will always be a level of uncertainty. Uncertainty avoidance refers to how the comfort level of members of a certain culture might change in various situations that don't seem to have any structure.

4. In order to make sure an organization can meet its goal, a certain level of human resources are needed to help meet the objectives. The process of analyzing and identifying how much human resources are needed is known as:

    A. Operational organizations

    B. Human resource planning

    C. Strategic organizational management

    D. Managerial organization

Answer - B - The process of analyzing and identifying how much human resources is needed is known as human resource planning. This helps to make sure an organization can meet its goal while determining how much human resources is needed to meet the objectives.

Explanation and key takeaway: An HRM is responsible for looking over all other staff and making sure their needs are taken care of, they're being compensated, and all rules are being followed in order to make sure that things continue to run smoothly. However, an HRM is also responsible for themselves! They have to make sure that they are identifying the need for human resources, what the might require in the future, and how different costs could be cut in their own department. Human resource planning is important in connecting the overall organization to the actual human resources.

5. When there is a reduction in size of the overall workforce of an organization, it is referred to as:

   A. Layoff

   B. Outsourcing

   C. Downsizing

D. Training

Answer - C - Downsizing is when there is a reduction in size of the overall workforce of an organization.

Explanation and key takeaway: Downsizing can occur for many different reasons. It might be to cut costs for a struggling company. It might also be used as a way to increase profit instead, by looking at positions that don't hold as much value as others. Downsizing can also happen during moments of rebranding, when computers or other services are used in place of positions previously held by employees.

Downsizing a staff can affect not only those that have to lose their jobs, but also the employees that are left. They might fear that they are next in line to get cut, or they might have trouble taking on new responsibilities that the former employees left behind. The decision to downsize is not made by the HRM, but it is up to them to make sure that this operation goes smoothly, and no one suffers more than they have to.

6. Organization development can be

divided between three different categories. Which is NOT one of the categories?

A. Technological

B. Interpersonal

C. Structural

D. Executive

Answer - D - Organization development can be divided between three different categories – technological, interpersonal, and structural.

Explanation and key takeaway: Organization development refers to what it sounds like – how to develop organizational practices within a business. It starts with a technological aspect: What can be computerized, digitized, or uploaded to an online storage system? How can technology improve overall organization and the work efforts of the different employees? The next stage is interpersonal: What is going on with the employees of a company that can be changed to be better organized? Finally, a structural standpoint should be established for HRMs that want to achieve better organization development: What overall, in the structure of the company, needs to be developed in order to achieve optimal organization?

Strategy

This last section in the first part of the book is going to go over everything else within business management and strategy that might not have already been covered.

1. What are the dimensions taken from Hofstede's IBM employee study?

   A. Uncertainty avoidance, long-term orientation, power distance, individualism, and management commitment

   B. Uncertainty avoidance, long-term orientation, power distance, individualism, and masculine/feminine

   C. Uncertainty avoidance, internal standards, orientation, power distance, individualism, and management commitment

D. Internal standards, orientation, power distance, individualism, masculine/feminine, and management commitment

Answer - B - The five dimensions taken from Hofstede's IBM employee study are: uncertainty avoidance, long-term orientation, power distance, individualism, and masculine/feminine.

Explanation and key takeaway: Hofstede's IBM employee study aimed to see how different cultures were affected by systematic differences. His analysis produced four dimensions on which national cultures differentiated. The first was uncertainty avoidance. This is how comfortable certain people are with change, or the uncertainty level of different aspects of life. The second is long-term orientation, or how someone might plan for the future. The third is power distance, which is how others influence those around them, and to what level they're comfortable doing so: How willing are people to accept inequality? The fourth is individualism, which is all about personal needs and whether or not someone's personal goals are being met versus the overall goals of the organization. The final dimension is masculine/feminine, which looks at how masculine and feminine rules determine different cultural aspects.

2. There are certain stages of a lifecycle of Human Resource Development. Which is not an example of a stage?

   A. Growth

   B. Maturity

   C. Middle age

   D. Introduction

Answer - C - Of the stages of a lifecycle of human resource development, middle age is not one of them. Growth, maturity, and introduction are all considered stages.

Explanation and key takeaway: Much like a business lifecycle, a human resource development lifecycle has similar stages. They begin with an introduction, where an HRM is aware of their responsibilities and introduces others to these methods as well. The second stage is growth, when different aspects of the HRM role are smoothed over. The next stage is maturity, when peak management is reached, and instead of dying off like a business cycle, there is a level of management that is maintained, with certain standards in place that are concrete and secure.

3. A "prospector" organization would include this type of HR practice:

   A. External staffing

   B. Promotion of business

   C. Conflict resolution

   D. Extensive training

Answer - A - An organization that would be considered a "prospector" would include the HR practice of external staffing.

Explanation and key takeaway: External staffing is when employees are recruited from outside of a company to fill necessary positions, rather than looking within a company. This is different than just hiring for an open position. Sometimes, it means looking elsewhere for a manager rather than at a staff that might have years of experience. A company that is a "prospector" is one that is looking for innovations and new ways to boost their product or service. They might consider external staffing as a way to bring fresh life into a company that desperately needs a change.

4. Which of the following choices best describes Succession Plans?

   A. A layout of an employer's mission statement, employment requirements, and other legal documents needed in the hiring process

   B. An anticipation of the staffing requirements a managerial position holds, with a development of high-quality employees in order to meet these needs stated

   C. A plan for what will happen should an HR manager face a strike from a union

   D. A plan that states who will move into a managerial position should the current position holder experience death or illness

Answer - B - Succession Plans can be described as an anticipation of the staffing requirements a managerial position holds, with a development of high-quality employees in order to meet these needs stated.

Explanation and key takeaway: HR Succession Planning looks at employees that can fill the positions of those in a managerial position when they can no longer fulfill their duties. This might mean setting others up to take over when someone quits or retires. By using proper succession planning, HRMs can make transitions smooth when those who might have held a certain position for decades finally leaves. New management can be very tricky for many businesses to recover from, but is something that can be implemented without much destruction if there is a proper succession plan in place.

5. HRIS stands for:

    A. Human Resource Information System

    B. Human Resource Information Succession

    C. Human Resource Institutional System

    D. Human Resource Information Steps

Answer - A - HRIS stands for Human Resource Information System.

Explanation and key takeaway: This might also be known as a Human Resource Management System (HRMS). This refers to the software and technology used by HRMs. There is not one specific program necessary for all HRMs to use, though there are certain favorites. It's important to know the acronym in order to determine if a technological or interpersonal issue is being discussed in terms of strategic human resource management. Having electronic HR management documentations allows for certain managers to better look over past and future proceedings to ensure that no steps are being missed, and all information is presented.

6. Which of the following is NOT part of the development of a business strategy?

    A. Employee dislikes

    B. Internal scan

    C. External scan

    D. All of these are part of a business strategy

**Answer - A - ** The dislikes of an employee are not part of the development of a business strategy.

Explanation and key takeaway: When developing a business strategy, it is important to look at both the external factors that might threaten a business, as well as the internal systems that could provide strengths and weaknesses to a company. An external scan might include things like environmental factors, demographics, competitors, and basic geographical locations. Internal scanning requires businesses to look inward, seeing what weaknesses might hold them back. These could be things such as not having enough of a budget, lack of experience, or the unavailability of certain resources. These two scans are very important in producing a quality business strategy.

Part 2 – Workforce Planning and Employment

The second part of the practice questions book is going to go over Workforce Planning and Employment. This might include anything from how an employee gets hired, to the job description that is needed for initial recruitment.

1. Which is considered employment discrimination?

    A. Sex discrimination

    B. Racial/ethnic discrimination

    C. Age discrimination

    D. All are valid forms of discrimination

Answer - D - Sex, racial/ethnic, and age discrimination are all considered types of employment discrimination.

Explanation and key takeaway: Discrimination comes in many different forms. It is sometimes obvious, and other times challenging to identify. An experienced HRM will know how to spot discrimination and what makes up a discriminatory act. If any discrimination is even sensed, it is always worth investigating. Those that are discriminated against belong to a protected class, which includes, women, minorities, and those part of the LGBTQA community. Discrimination could be as subtle as not giving a requested vacation day to someone in a protected group, or it could be as large as firing someone because they are homosexual. No matter the degree of discrimination that an employee faces, action must be taken by an HRM to protect the worker's rights and the integrity of the company.

2. Employee evaluation is also known as:

   A. Performance appraisal

   B. Job design

   C. HR strategic management

   D. 360-degree feedback

Answer - **A** - Performance appraisal is another way of saying "employee evaluation." Job design, HR strategic management, and

360-degree feedback all refer to different things, but none mean the same thing as an employee evaluation.

Explanation and key takeaway: In a performance appraisal, an employee's contribution to the company, as well as overall job performance, will be evaluated. Because this is similar to an employee evaluation, the two terms can be interchangeable. Sometimes, these reviews might happen annually, or they could happen every month. Sometimes, reviews will be face to face, but they also might be completed through documents. The point of doing a performance evaluation is to ensure there aren't any problems that need addressing between management and an employee. Areas of strength and weakness can be discussed in a performance review, allowing for both the company and the employee to continually grow.

There are three key functions that must be addressed in a performance appraisal. The first one being feedback. This needs to be provided to both the employee and the employer: What does each think of the others' performance? The second key function is to allow for modification of working habits or a work environment. The third function is one that provides data to the manager and the HRM that can be used for future assessment. It gives a basis for comparison so that each job assessment becomes more functional.

3. If an employer only hires young, thin, attractive women, they are exhibiting:

   A. Sexual harassment

   B. Intentional treatment

   C. Disparate treatment

   D. None of the above

Answer - C - Hiring only young, thin, attractive women can be a form of disparate treatment. Sexual harassment and intentional treatment might also be exhibited in addition to this, but they aren't necessarily inherent of the same things as disparate treatment.

Explanation and key takeaway: Disparate treatment is when there is an intentional discrimination in the employment process. It might involve testing certain sexes or minorities in different areas rather than testing all employees equally. Someone that wants to only give background checks to African American applicants would be practicing disparate treatment.

Disparate impact occurs when there is more of an unintentional discriminatory practice in place. A disparate impact is one that might eliminate a certain protected group during the interview process because of a requirement that would likely make them ineligible. For example, imagine an electrician who's reaching the age of retirement, but he's not ready to end his career. The electrician's managers fire him and justify doing so because he received several complaints. They are allowed to fire him, however, if there are several other employees that are younger than him with the same amount of complaints, and the company doesn't fire them, they are exhibiting a disparate impact.

4. Which of these is an alternative work schedule?

    A. Self-employment

    B. Remote

    C. Job sharing

    D. Self-directed task force

Answer - C - Job sharing is an example of an alternative work schedule. Self-employment, self-directed task force, and remote are all terms that have different meanings than "alternative work schedule."

Explanation and key takeaway: An alternative work schedule is one that includes a full workweek completed in a condensed amount of time. Instead of working a full 40-hour workweek within five days, it might be completed in three. Any form of a compressed work schedule would be considered alternative.

Job sharing is in reference to more than one employee that shares the duties of a full-time position. For example, two people might work 20-hours within a three-day period, completing the tasks that someone might have needed 5 days for if it were one full-time employee. Working remotely could be considered an alternative work schedule, but only if that employee chooses to do their full-time work within a short period of time.

5. Which of the following answers best describes an index number that is given to the relationship between a predictor and the criterion variable?

A. Predictive validity

B. Content coefficient

C. Correlation validity

D. Correlation coefficient

Answer - A - Predictive validity best describes an index number that is given to the relationship between a predictor and the criterion variable.

Explanation and key takeaway: As an HRM, it is important to understand all the ways that different employee data analytics can be predicted and analyzed. Depending on an HRM's objective, there is likely going to be a different method of achieving the desired information. Sometimes, this information isn't going to be completely accurate, but in other instances, it might have uses.

Predictive validity refers to the efficiency in which a test is conducted and the information that is measured. Predictive validity looks at how that tool was used to achieve the desired information, and whether or not it did the job it needed to do. By doing this assessment, it can be better determined how results might be best achieved the next time an HRM is collecting data.

6. Which is NOT included in a job analysis?

 A. A way to gather information about the content of a job

 B. The context in which jobs are performed

 C. A systematic method of analyzing human requirements

 D. All of the above

Answer - D - A job analysis would include investigating a way to gather information about the content of a job, a systematic method of analyzing human requirements, and the context in which jobs are performed.

Explanation and key takeaway: In a job analysis, the certain duties required by a position are identified. It looks at what duties, jobs, specifications, and responsibilities of a position are important in order to collect data and analyze what parts of a position are required, and which can be cut down: Is a person getting paid enough, or is there a way that hours could be cut in order to save money?

By figuring out an in-depth job analysis, HRMs are able to decide who is the best fit for a certain position, and who would be better suited elsewhere. A job analysis differs from a job description in that it is more in-depth, and a process performed by an HRM, while a job description would simply list the duties and expectations of a certain position.

7. An independent contractor:

    A. Is flexible in their scheduling

    B. Maintains continuous relationships with their employers

    C. Has to provide their own tools.

    D. A and C

Answer - D - An independent contractor is flexible in their scheduling and has to provide their own tools. An independent contractor will not always maintain continuous relationships with their employers.

Explanation and key takeaway: An independent contractor is someone that is contracted by an employer for a certain duty, task, operation, or goal. They are hired on as a non-employee and are only brought in to take on that certain task. Sometimes, an independent contractor might work for a company more than once if the employer likes their work. For example, someone working at a video production company might get hired to help light sets, but they wouldn't be given a consistent position and would instead continue to find their own work elsewhere. They would likely bring some of their own lights and would have to make sure all their projects would allow for a new position to be taken on. They might never hear from the employer again for another project, or they might get hired every other month when their work is needed.

8. What does the FLSA regulate?

    A. Overtime pay, record keeping, administrative concerns, and employee status

    B. The retirement plans of employees

    C. Work-related injuries that might have caused an employee to have to take out worker's compensation

D. The family affairs of an employee

Answer - A - The FLSA regulates overtime pay, recordkeeping, administrative concerns, and employee status. The FLSA is not responsible for the retirement plans of employees, work-related injuries that might have caused an employee to take out worker's compensation, or the familial affairs of their employees.

Explanation and key takeaway: According to the United States Department of Labor's website, "The Fair Labor Standards Act (FLSA) establishes minimum wage, overtime pay, recordkeeping, and child labor standards affecting full-time and part-time workers in the private sector and in Federal, State, and local governments." This would protect any overtime pay that an employee deserves, and the record keeping involved in their employment history. It would also include administrative concerns, as well as an employee's status, in reference to if they are part-time, temporary, or on a working visa.

The FLSA does not include any retirement plans, as that would be more between the relationship with the employee and their employer, or with a different independent retirement plan they are working with.

9. What is a closed shop?

    A. A store that is not open for business

    B. A union that requires hired employees to join the union upon hiring

    C. A union that does not allow any new union members

    D. A union that no longer exists

Answer - B - A closed shop refers to a union that requires hired employees to join the union upon hiring. It does not refer to an old union, a closed store, or a union that does not allow any new members.

Explanation and key takeaway: In a closed shop, there will be a predetermined agreement between the union and employers in which they will only hire those that are going to become union members. Employees must also remain a member of that union, meaning from beginning to end, they are in agreement with their union. By doing this, it keeps the union stronger and allows for the union to also have more of a say in who is a good candidate to hire.

Not all unions work this way, so it is important to know all of the different kinds of unions and what agreements come along with each different type of union shop.

10. What type of interview uses questions to investigate what an employee might have done in other positions that are related to the job being interviewed for?

   A. Group interview

   B. Phone interview

   C. Situational interview

   D. Targeted-selection interview

Answer - D - A targeted-selection interview uses questions to investigate what an employee might have done in other positions that are related to the job being interviewed for. A group, phone, and situational interview all use different methods of gaining information about potential candidates.

Explanation and key takeaway: A target-selection interview allows the employer to determine the specific points of a job and how well a person might be able to fulfill those duties. In a target-selection interview, the previous jobs and duties that someone went through in their past positions will provide examples of how they might perform in the next position. Not only does this allow an employer to better determine if the person they are interviewing is right for the position, but the potential candidate also has the opportunity to meet management and see if the job is really something that they are interested in after all.

These are common types of interviews, though there are many others that have their own benefits as well. It's important to go into the test knowing about all the different types of interviews in order to be fully prepared.

11. What is included in a job description?

   A. Working conditions

   B. Reporting relationships

   C. Duties

D. All of the above

Answer - D - A job description might include working conditions, reporting relationships, and duties.

> **Explanation and key takeaway:** A job description is necessary in order to weed out potential candidates that wouldn't be a good fit for a position. At any given time, there are many people on the hunt for a new job. Not every single one of these people is going to be a good fit, or even qualified, for certain positions. The more detailed a job description, the better the chance that the applicants will be good candidates for interview.
>
> A job description will list the responsibilities of that position, and their purpose and relation to other positions in the company. How often someone is interacting with the public or working in a team will usually be specified in a job description as well. The qualifications needed, whether it's a degree, certificate, or number of years of experience will also help make a job description more detailed, to ensure that only those that qualify will be able to get an interview slot. A job description might include a potential

salary, though this is often something that is going to be discussed after the first interview when abilities are determined.

12. "This for that," also means:

    A. Quid pro quo

    B. Sympathy

    C. Whistleblowing

    D. Reasonable person

Answer - A - A quid pro quo can also mean "this for that." Sympathy, whistleblowing, and reasonable person are all terms that have different meanings.

Explanation and key takeaway: A quid pro quo is a favor that is given, but with the expectation that same favor will be returned or repaid in another way. "This for that," is another way to explain this, as you might say, "if you give me this, I'll give you that." In terms of human resource management, this is something that has to be familiar in order to ensure it is not taking place in the workplace. Most often, a quid pro quo is seen when a manager offers something to an employee in return for a sexual, or otherwise illegal, favor. This form of harassment can be very dangerous, as the employee might feel fearful to tell the HRM of the harassment out of fear of losing their job. Unfortunately, a quid pro quo is the most common form of harassment in different work environments.

Part 3 – Total Rewards

Total Rewards refer to the compensation, salary, wage, benefits, and other bonuses that employees are entitled to. The payroll is how these employees are going to be getting the money that they are owed. This part is split into three sections, each just as important to know as the other before going in for the test.

Compensation

Compensation might include anything from workman's comp to maternity leave. There are many different forms of compensation, as well as the methods in which it is received. There are different laws and organizations that protect a worker's right to certain compensation, so it is important to make yourself aware of all compensation aspects before completing the questions in this section.

1. A form of indirect compensation can be represented by:

   A. Merit pays

B. Unpaid leave

C. Social security benefits

D. Differential pay

Answer - C - Social security benefits would all be forms of indirect compensation. Merit pays, unpaid leave, and differential pay are all considered to be something else.

> **Explanation and key takeaway:** Indirect compensation is a way of stating benefits. The bonuses that come along with a company would be referred to as the indirect benefits that are associated with a certain position. Unpaid leave, social security benefits, and differential pay would all present themselves in cash or check form. Indirect compensation might be the price taken off a medical bill that was covered by insurance, or a bonus like a company car or phone that the employee can use at their own discretion. Different forms of indirect compensation should be known in order to better pass the test.

2. When it comes to compensation associated with discrimination, which of the following will work directly with this issue to solve a problem?

A. Davis-Bacon Act

B. Fair Labor Standards Act

C. McCormick Act

D. Equal Pay Act

Answer - D - The Equal Pay Act will help with compensation associated with discrimination.

Explanation and key takeaway: According to the U.S. Equal Employment Opportunity Commission, the Equal Pay Act of 1963, "prohibits sex-based wage discrimination between men and women in the same establishment who perform jobs that require substantially equal skill, effort, and responsibility under similar working conditions." This was enacted in 1963 in order to protect the rights of workers. Though dates can sometimes be hard to memorize, the test often asks for different dates as a way to test memorization skills of the test taker.

3. Which of the following would be addressed in a compensation program?

A. Cost-Effectiveness

B. Legal compliance

C. Equity for employees

D. All of the above

Answer - D - Legal compliance, equity for employees, and cost-effectiveness might all be factors that would be addressed in a compensation program.

> **Explanation and key takeaway:** A compensation program would include how and what an employee is going to be paid. It might include any legal compliance that the company would cover for their employees. There is also a chance that it would consider different equity for employees, as well as the cost-effectiveness of certain other programs that exist within the compensation plan.
>
> An HRM would be responsible for overlooking different compensation programs and would have to be sure that they are creating something cost-efficient and fair enough to cover what the employee is entitled to.

4. Which of the following best describes what is received by executives?

   A. More variety regarding available compensation programs, as compared to the other employees in the firm

B. A strict flat rate among the top ten highest paid employees in a company

C. A paycheck exempt from federal taxes

D. Compensation paid quarterly

Answer - A - Executives receive more variety regarding available compensation programs, as compared to the other employees in the firm. Executives do not receive a strict flat rate among the top ten highest paid employees in a company, nor do they receive a paycheck exempt from federal taxes. An executive might get compensation paid quarterly, but this is not necessarily an executive standard.

Explanation and key takeaway: Executives are paid much differently because there is usually an element of incentive involved for the executive to perform, or to encourage their staff to perform, more efficiently to turn a higher profit. Long-term cash incentives are involved in executive corporations, as well as global compensation. There is no standard for an executive compensation program, but it will typically involve many more benefits and luxuries than other employees in the company. The pay packages are much more diverse, and it's important to know what might be involved in order to differentiate from other employee compensation programs.

5. Out of the following answers, which would be described as a form of direct compensation?

    A. Long-term incentive pay

    B. Maternity leave

    C. Flexible benefits

    D. Worker's compensation

Answer - A - Long-term incentive pay is best described as a form of direct compensation. Maternity leave, flexible benefits, and worker's compensation are all forms of compensation, but are not direct.

Explanation and key takeaway: Direct compensation refers to any instance when money is directly paid to an employee. Most often, this includes salaries, wages, commission, and bonuses. Indirect payment involves something that isn't liquid, paid to an employee. This would include maternity leave, other flexible benefits, and worker's compensation.

Long-term incentive pay refers to any time an executive is paid for achieving certain goals or milestones. These usually include strategic objectives and performance goals that will motivate the executive to increase profit throughout the company, therefore promising long-term incentive pay. What makes up a long-term incentive pay program differs, but it is still referred to as a form of direct compensation.

6. Under the Fair Labor Standards Act, an employee that holds a non-exempt position is someone that:

    A. Performs clerical, routine, or manual work during a percentage of their time

    B. Has an annual income of less than $45,000

    C. Holds a managerial position and expects to be promoted within the next six months

    D. Both A and C

Answer - A - Non-exempt positions, according to the Fair Labor Standards Act, would be positions that perform clerical, routine, or manual work during a percentage of their time.

Explanation and key takeaway: Most employees are protected by the FLSA, meaning they are non-exempt. Non-exempt positions are entitled to overtime pay. If more than 40 hours of work are given in a pay week, that employee is entitled to pay that is at least time and a half, though some companies might have different overtime incentives. Either way, the FLSA mandates that non-exempt employees receive what they deserve when overtime work is given. Exempt employees are those that earn a salary of $23,660 per year, or more. These workers are not protected under the FLSA, though many companies will still offer overtime pay if a certain number of hours are worked, as an employee incentive.

Payroll

Payroll refers to how someone gets paid. They might receive monthly checks, or they could get a weekly direct deposit. The wages, salaries, hourly rates, and paychecks of employees, as well as the laws to protect them, are important to be aware of as an HRM, to ensure that all compensation and benefits are being properly provided.

1. A _____ is a form of payment that remains consistent each and every period, not dependent on the number of hours worked.

   A. Rate per hour

   B. Reward

   C. Salary

   D. Wage

Answer - C - A salary refers to a form of payment that remains consistent each and every period, not dependent on the number of hours worked.

Explanation and key takeaway: Many employees are given a salary, which is usually an amount slightly higher than what the average total amount of a 40-hour minimum wage paycheck would be. A salary is usually referred to in annual terms, meaning if a person gets paid $1,000 per week, they have a salary of $52,000 per year. This form of payment is mostly given to professional and white-collar workers. Not everyone in a company gets paid the same, so some employees might make a salary while others receive an hourly fee. Getting paid a salary will usually be part of a compensation package that also includes other benefits, such as paid vacation, healthcare, and other forms of insurance.

2. In one week at a hotel, a maid worked 30 hours and took 12 vacation hours, a non-exempt security guard put in 45 hours total, and a front desk clerk worked 40 hours, 10 of which were on Christmas. Which employee would get overtime?

   A. The security guard

   B. The front desk clerk

   C. The maid

   D. All of them must be paid overtime.

Answer - A – The security guard would be

considered non-exempt out of all the employees listed.

Explanation and key takeaway: If someone partially works their weekly hours as well as a combination of cashing in on vacation hours for their weekly salary, they wouldn't be entitled to overtime, even if they got paid for more than forty hours in a week. For example, someone that works 39 hours in a week and uses 2 vacation hours would not be entitled to that extra hour of overtime pay, since the hours weren't technically worked. Getting paid time and a half doesn't qualify as overtime either. Overtime is only given when someone actually works more than forty hours in a week, and they are non-exempt. There might be situational examples on the test that could slip up some takers, so it's important to be aware of how to apply these rules and laws to real-life situations.

3. The Davis-Bacon Act of 1931 is most relevant to companies that:

   A. Are firms currently engaged with federal construction projects, and only those whose projects exceed the cost of $2,000. This also states that the "prevailing wage," is a rate that must be paid.

B. Have a high number of expectant mothers that might be taking time off at the same time

C. Are particularly dangerous and make workers more susceptible to earning worker's compensation

D. Pay their employees under the table for religious purposes

Answer - A - The Davis-Bacon Act of 1931 is most relevant to companies that are firms currently engaged with federal construction projects, and only those whose projects exceed the cost of $2,000. This also states that the "prevailing wage," is a rate that must be paid.

Explanation and key takeaway: The Davis-Bacon Act is important in protecting federal workers, ensuring that they are entitled to minimum wage standards even when not working full-time positions. This Act emerged in 1931 and states that those protected are "contractors and subcontractors performing on federally funded or assisted contracts in excess of $2,000 for the construction, alteration, or repair (including painting and decorating) of public buildings or public works."

4. The Hay system is composed of which three main factors?

  A. Experience, problem-solving, accountability

  B. Problem-solving, know-how, accountability

  C. Problem-solving, know-how, experience

  D. Accountability, know-how, experience

Answer - B - The Hay System is composed of problem-solving, know-how, and accountability. It does not include experience.

Explanation and key takeaway: The hay system puts an emphasis on problem-solving, making sure that every step is met to resolve a conflict. It also references know-how and accountability. Experience is not looked at, as that is more of an external factor.

5. A person-based pay system can be best described as:

  A. Paying employees more often

with short-term service

B. A system that is impossible to use with large companies

C. A system that doesn't pay employees based on the tasks that are currently performing, but rather based on what the employees are capable of doing

D. A system that depends on an employee tracking their own hours and healthcare

Answer - C - A system that doesn't pay employees based on the tasks that are currently performing, but rather based on what employees are capable of doing is known as a person-based pay system.

> **Explanation and key takeaway:** A person-based pay system might involve an employee getting paid more based on the experience or skill level that they have. This might also include getting paid more based on a certification or degree that someone has. It cannot be based on any sort of discriminatory reasons, such as a person's age or sex.

6. The Equal Pay Act was put in place in

order to make sure that those with the same skills, effort, and responsibilities are protected. There are some exemptions, which are listed below except WHICH of the following?

A. Overtime

B. Experience

C. Seniority

D. Gender

Answer - A - An exemption from The Equal Pay act would be overtime.

Explanation and key takeaway: The Equal Pay act was put in place in order to make sure that everyone would be paid fairly in an organization, no matter their race, sex, age, or any other reason that someone might discriminate against them. However, there are some exceptions that define that certain differences in pay aren't considered wage discrimination. One exception is seniority pay. This means that certain people that were in a company longer than others are entitled to a higher pay because of their seniority. A merit system is another exemption from a different wage gap, meaning that an employee's job performance will determine how they might get paid. Certain factors within these exemptions might be subjective, which is where the importance of an HRM comes in to make sure that the exemption is legitimate.

Benefits

Benefits include any additional compensation that an employee is entitled to. For some, this includes healthcare, dental care, vision plans, vacation pay, and other bonuses that are of different monetary values than hourly rate or salary. Every company is different in terms of the benefits that employees are offered, but there is still plenty of general information that needs to be known by HRMs, so they can ensure that their employees are receiving proper benefits.

1. While it is morally just to offer a benefits package to an employee, it also presents a strategic business reason in that it:

    A. Helps to attract and maintain a high level of employment

B. Makes the company look better than competitors

C. Makes employees healthier and less grumpy to work with

D. Offers a cost-effective way to feed employees

Answer - A - Offering a benefits package to an employee will help attract and maintain a high level of employment.

Explanation and key takeaway: Compensation in the form of a benefits package can be great for the employee. For example, having insurance brings peace of mind, as well as many other factors that would improve a worker's mood while working. Apart from benefits to the employee, there is also a good reason for a company to offer their employees a fair benefits package. The main reason would be to help reduce turnover. Employees that are satisfied with the amount they are receiving and the protection that surrounds their health as well of their families will be more likely to stick around, meaning that recruitment and training costs can go down.

2. The services and costs billed by certain health-care providers is an audit that is referred to as:

    A. Practice analysis

    B. Utilization review

    C. Organizational control

    D. Procedural analysis

Answer - B - Utilization review is an audit that consists of the services and costs billed by certain health-care providers.

> **Explanation and key takeaway:** While many different aspects of a health insurance plan can benefit an employee, the health-care provider might not always accept it. A utilization review is the chance for a health insurance company to look over the different requests for medical treatment that an employee might have submitted. Sometimes, a recommended treatment might not be the appropriate one to go through with, so in some cases, an HRM might have to work with insurance agents to determine whether or not certain aspects of health-care are required after all.

3. Of the below, which would NOT be

considered a legally mandated benefit?

A. Social security

B. Worker's compensation

C. Holiday bonuses

D. Unemployment compensation

Answer - C - Holiday bonuses would not be considered legally mandated benefits. Social security, worker's compensation, and unemployment compensation would all be considered legally mandated benefits.

Explanation and key takeaway: Legally-mandated benefits, also known as legally required benefits, are anything that is required to cover the treatment of different aspects of health-care. These might include social security, Medicare, or those outlined by the Federal Insurance Contributions Act (FICA). This is what's often taken out of employee's checks in order to go to other services. Holiday bonuses and other forms of compensation that are "extra" features would not be considered legally mandated benefits. You can remember this by thinking of those whose basic needs have to be taken care of. Lower-income families, the elderly, and those that are disabled still need to receive money, which is where legally-mandated benefits would come in.

4. Different health plans have various funding features. Which of the below would best fit in as one?

   A. PTO coverage

   B. Doctors' visits

   C. HMO compensation

   D. Self-insurance

Answer - D - Self-insurance is an example of a funding feature that might be found in a health plan.

> **Explanation and key takeaway:** Self-insurance is when an employee might decide not to avail of company health insurance, and rather cover their own costs. They might not get any insurance at all, though with the Affordable Care Act, this isn't supposed to present itself as an option anymore.

5. If an employee is experiencing emotional, physical, or other personal problems, which program provides

counseling, or any other help that the employee might need?

A. OSHA

B. Employee assistance programs

C. The Stanley Dudley Act of 1987

D. Wellness programs

Answer - B - Employee assistance programs help those that are experiencing emotional, physical, or other personal problems within a company.

Explanation and key takeaway: Employee assistance programs, which also might be referred to as EAPs, are voluntary and work-based programs that offer assessments, counseling, and referrals, and are usually anonymous. These programs might be used by someone who is experiencing work or personal problems. These programs are paid for by the employers and allow them to make sure that any issues that are affecting their employees can be properly taken care of to ensure that there is no hold-up in the work process.

Part 4 – Training and Development

Training and Development refers to any part of a company that is involved with training their employees. This is one of the most important parts of a business lifecycle. An HRM should know all about how to properly train employees and what the best methods might be. The development of training programs is important as well. HRMs need to make sure they have the proper analytic and data tools to determine if their methods of training are productive or actually hurting the company and causing high turnover.

1. Training is defined as:

    A. Learning skills that apply to an employee during the current job

    B. An individual learning experience, in a general sense

    C. Preparation for an employee's future career

    D. The education required to get a

certain degree

Answer - A - Training is defined as learning skills that apply to an employee during the current job. Individual learning experience, preparation for an employee's future career, and the education required to get a certain degree would not be considered training in terms of an HR position.

Explanation and key takeaway: Training is the process in which an employee gains a particular new set of skills and tools that will be applicable to their time employed with the company. An HRM is responsible for setting up an employee's training, but they might not always be the ones in charge of making sure that an employee is trained. For some companies, an HRM will also look at the learning skills that apply to an employee during the current job and figure out whether or not training programs are efficient. An HRM will work with those that train others to make sure that the process is going as smoothly as possible, so as to make sure the new employee can start regular work as soon as possible, without compromising the learning of any important skills that will help the company improve and grow.

2. Which best applies to all four phases of
the learning process?

   A. Reaction

   B. Results

   C. Behavior

   D. Questioning

Answer - D - Questioning best applies to all four phases of the learning process.

Explanation and key takeaway: For some companies, the four phases of learning might differ a bit, but there are certain key elements that can be seen in four different steps. The first involves unconscious competence, which might include a form of preparation. Inciting interest in the company might also be included in this first step. It might involve a trainer going over what is involved in the day-day operation of a certain business with the new employee.

The second stage of learning is coming face-to-face with these new skills, which is when hands-on training might start. The third would be application, and using this new knowledge or set of skills to actually go out there and begin working. The final stage would be using these skills regularly without any practice. In all of the stages, questioning is the most important in order to make sure the employee is constantly learning.

3. Which of these best describes an instance in which an error occurs based on prejudice in a rater's score?

    A. Raters bias

    B. Leniency

    C. Tendency

    D. All of these

Answer - A - Rater's bias is an instance in which an error occurs based on prejudice in a rater's score.

Explanation and key takeaway: If someone is making a judgment, for instance, in a job interview, a rating might be done, and that judgment lets their personal interest affect their professional score, this would be known as a rater's bias. As an HRM, it is crucial that personal ideas don't interfere with a rating that might be given to an employee on a professional level. For instance, if an employee has a certain tattoo of a band that the HRM doesn't like, this should not affect the way they perceive that employee. If tattoos are permitted, nothing about the personal taste of that employee should affect how an HRM treats them, so during an employee review, small personal distaste among the two should be kept out of the equation. If not, a rater's bias might occur, giving the employee an unfair disadvantage.

4. KSA is:

   A. Knowledge, skill, and accountability

   B. Knowledge, service, and action

   C. Knowledge, skill, and ability

   D. Knowledge, social, and ability

Answer - C - Knowledge, skill, and ability are the words in the acronym KSA.

Explanation and key takeaway: KSA is often used when discussing job duties, evaluations, descriptions, and anything else that might be included in an overall job analysis. The knowledge is what needs to be known by an employee, either through previous experience or the training that they're going to partake in. Skill involves the set of skills that might be needed by a particular employee in order to ensure that the job is completed. Ability is all about the performance of the employee, whether it's through the expected requirements or through a description of what abilities they might have to have.

5. Which of the following can best describe the duties and tasks performed by those in training?

    A. Training practice

    B. Active practice

    C. Spaced practice

    D. Specialized practice

Answer - B - Active practice refers to the duties and tasks performed by those in training.

Explanation and key takeaway: Those that are in training go through different stages of learning. It might start with just shadowing someone, for example, in a serving setting. They would follow a staff member around as they wait on tables, making sure to keep in mind the duties and responsibilities they're witnessing, and use this for a basis of what they're going to do when training has ended. After that, they might start actually waiting tables themselves, but still with the help of a trained staff member. This would be referred to as active practice. They are actually taking the skills that they have learned in training so far and actively applying them to the job duties that lie ahead.

6. Which below shows the impact that physical and environmental influence has on employee performance, and in some cases, how special notice from a managerial position could help increase motivation in an employee:

    A. The Hawthorne studies

    B. Group dynamics

    C. McKinley-Hill theory

    D. Training procedure

Answer - A – The Hawthorne studies show the impact that physical and environmental influence has on employee performance, and in some cases, how special notice from a managerial position could help increase motivation in an employee

Explanation and key takeaway: The Hawthorne studies are a set of ideas and practices that were studied in Cicero, Illinois at the Hawthorne Works. This study proved that some employees might alter their work if they are aware that they are being watched. The original idea went on to inspire other work-related discoveries, including how a physical and environmental space might affect the employee that's working within that space.

7. What was the point of the Hawthorne studies?

   A. To figure out who might have communist intentions

   B. To understand how criminals get along in the workplace

   C. To figure out how to rehabilitate injured workers back into the workforce

   D. To determine how workers interact in a certain environment

Answer - D - The point of the Hawthorne studies was to determine how workers interact in a certain environment.

Explanation and key takeaway: The point of these studies was to focus on workers' needs, and they did just that, igniting more studies to determine the best way to keep employees happy and efficient. An HRM should be familiar with the results of the Hawthorne Studies as well as other instances of workers' behavior being observed. The more that is known about the scientific reason a worker might act the way they do, the better prepared an HRM is to find a solution to help resolve any issues that might arise, whether they're personal or professional.

8. Which one is NOT a strategy used as a behavior modification approach?

   A. Punishment

   B. Negative reinforcement

   C. Positive reinforcement

   D. Behavior modeling

Answer - D - Behavior modeling is not a strategy used as a behavior modification approach.

Explanation and key takeaway: An HRM needs to be aware of different behavior modification approaches in order to determine how to possibly resolve a conflict. Whether this arises during training or with an employee that has been around a long time, there are different behavior modification approaches that need to be used in order to remedy various situations. Punishment might need to be taken, but only in forms of reprimand. That might include moving someone to a different position or cutting hours. Both negative and positive reinforcement could also help ensure that behavior changes, one way or the other.

9. If an employer wanted to discourage a certain behavior that they had continually tried to reprimand, what alternative method might be used to solve the issue of disobedience?

    A. Promotion

    B. Extinction

    C. Salting

    D. Mentoring

Answer - B - Extinction is when reinforcement for a particular negative behavior lessens so that the desire to break the rules doesn't occur. This practice is not used often.

> **Explanation and key takeaway:** Think of it like a child that keeps singing loudly just to be annoying. Instead of telling the child to stop, you just ignore the singing and hope that they realize they can no longer get a reaction out of you. It isn't always effective but can sometimes help when employees continually attempt to break the rules.

> 10. Which of the below is not considered a training needs analysis?
>
>> A. Organizational analysis
>>
>> B. Individual analysis
>>
>> C. Operations analysis
>>
>> D. Task analysis

Answer - C - Operations analysis is not considered a training needs analysis.

> **Explanation and key takeaway:** A training needs analysis would look at the

need for training versus employee training. It would identify if a problem could be fixed by further training, or if that would only make things worse in the end, possibly by spending too much time or money that could be better used elsewhere. Training needs analysis can be conducted using individual, task, or organizational analysis.

11. Employers receive direct costs for:

   A. Operating a unit

   B. Operating a department

   C. Operating a program

   D. Operating a strike

Answer - C - Operating a program is a cost directly received by employers.

   Explanation and key takeaway: A direct cost is one that can be traced directly to the production of a good or service. An indirect cost is one that is needed to keep the business in operation. Knowing both of these is important for an HRM so they can determine and price different costs, and budget accordingly.

12. Which selection would best describe a

job design practice that broadens the scope of a job?

A. Job enlargement

B. Rotation

C. Division of jobs

D. Division enrichments

Answer - A - Job enlargement is a job design practice that broadens the scope of a job.

Explanation and key takeaway: Job enlargement describes a technique in which there is an increase in the number of tasks that come along with a certain job. Some might assume that a job enlargement would be the process of increasing employees or the amount of work that a company is producing, but it's about the increase in work that is taken on by an individual. A job enlargement doesn't always necessarily mean a wage enlargement. Sometimes it's necessary for production, but other times it might be done to cut down costs or increase overall profit.

13. There are six levels of learning. Which of the below is NOT considered one of

them?

   A. Knowledge

   B. Analysis

   C. Apprenticeship

   D. Application

Answer - C - Apprenticeship is not considered a level of learning.

Explanation and key takeaway: Bloom's taxonomy describes the levels of learning in six different steps. The first one is knowledge. This is when previously known information is called upon in order for the advancement of more learning. Comprehension is second, which is when more is understood about what is being learned, while applying it to what is already known. The third is application, in which the first and second steps are applied to the new presentation at hand. The fourth level is analysis, in which what has been learned and what has yet to be learned are identified. The fifth is synthesis and the sixth is evaluation. It is important for HRMs to know these six steps in order to ensure that employees are learning in the proper and effective way, whether they're just starting a job or improving on the performance that they already give within a certain position.

14. The Hawthorne Study mainly focuses on:

    A. The personal relationships among employees

    B. Preparing employee reviews

    C. Analyzing and assessing how physical and environmental factors might affect performance

    D. Motivating employees to work harder

Answer - C - The Hawthorne Study mainly focuses on analyzing and assessing how physical and environmental factors might affect performance.

Explanation and key takeaway: The Hawthorne study puts emphasis on the socio-psychological aspects that might affect human behavior. This study was conducted within a workplace and provides employers with information about how their workers might react or handle certain things. The more an HRM knows about these important and monumental studies, the better they will be able to evaluate their own employees and ensure that both productivity and performance points are being consistently met at an above average level.

15. Which is NOT one of the three phases of training?

   A. Implementation

   B. Planning

   C. Job analysis

   D. Evaluation

Answer - C - Job analysis is not one of the three phases of training.

   Explanation and key takeaway: The three phases of training are planning, implementation, and evaluation. The first phase involves assessing an organization and its training needs. Different employees require different levels of training. The second step would be implementation, which is the process through which training would be done. This might include a weeklong training program, or one that's spread out over a few months. The third step would be evaluation, when it is determined whether this training method is effective or not. There are different processes within each of these steps, and they are all individually important to understand on their own level.

16. Which of the following is NOT a domain that influences change or behavior?

    A. Preparing

    B. Knowledge

    C. Skills

    D. Attitude

Answer - A - Preparing is not a domain that influences change or behavior.

Explanation and key takeaway: Knowledge, skills, and attitude are all domains that can influence both change and behavior. Knowledge of a certain subject will help in an analysis as well as a training procedure. A lack or surplus of knowledge can influence behavior, and is important in affecting change. The skills that someone has are also effective in eliciting change or influencing behavior. An attitude might just be the most important element for influencing behavior and eliciting change.

It is important to know the domains that can influence change and behavior in order to determine what methods are needed to effectively alter a workplace. It is up the HRM to look at their organization and be able to determine what change might be needed and how it can be achieved.

17. The four criteria for evaluating training programs are:

  A. Behavior, reactions, learning, and synthesis

  B. Behavior, reactions, time, and learning

  C. Interaction, reaction, progress, and learning

  D. Reaction, learning, behavior, and results

Answer - D - Reaction, learning, behavior, and results are the four criteria for evaluating training programs.

Explanation and key takeaway: In 1959, Donald Kirkpatrick created a model that could be used to effectively evaluate the methods of training that a particular company has. By using this model, HRM managers and trainers can look at their training methods objectively, and determine whether or not they are effective.

The first criterion in the model is reaction. This takes into account how people might feel about a training program and whether or not it is something they are comfortable with. The second criterion is learning: Are people actually learning something from this method of training? The third is behavior: Are people behaving differently than they did before the training programs? The fourth is results. This might include data analytics that looks at the results of a certain training method, in order to see if the program has actually made a difference.

18. When trainees are transferred to a different job in the hopes of broadening their focus, as well as increasing their knowledge, this is referred to as:

    A. Promotion

    B. Initiative learning

C. Job rotation

D. None of the above

Answer - C - Job rotation is when trainees are transferred to a different job in the hopes of broadening their focus, as well as increasing their knowledge.

> **Explanation and key takeaway:** Within certain companies, different tasks can be done by employees that have the same training. By moving around positions, employees get the opportunity to broaden their perspectives and look at what different opportunities there might be within a company. Sometimes, if production seems to be lacking or sales are low, an HRM might look at what employees could switch positions. By doing this, it might open up new opportunities for both the employees and the company. Someone in a retail store might be moved from ready-to-wear to jewelry, where they end up performing much better and drive sales even higher. This can benefit the company's profits and the satisfaction of the employee.

19. Which of the following is NOT related to the Hawthorne studies?

A. Assessing the impact of physical influence

B. Looking at the way environmental factors affect employees

C. A focus on how an employee's race might affect their position

D. All of these are part of the Hawthorne studies

Answer - C - A focus on how an employee's race might affect their position is not related to the Hawthorne studies.

Explanation and key takeaway: The Hawthorne studies aim to look at the impact of physical influence on a company. The physical conditions a job demands will directly affect the way an employee is performing. If they are in incredibly hot conditions all day, there's a good chance that they might not be the happiest employees. Part of the Hawthorne studies also look at the environmental factors that affect employees. Perhaps the company is located in a very cold area, so foot traffic might not be too high. Low sales could affect employee behavior, so this could be evaluated by the HRM. The Hawthorne studies look more at the things around different workers that can affect their performance, rather than the mental, socio-psychological factors.

20. Which of the following would be included in an employer's mission statement?

   A. Defining purpose, as well as laying out the values of an organization

   B. How much all positions pay

   C. The history of the company

   D. A legal agreement between an employee and an employer

Answer - A - Defining purpose, as well as laying out the values of an organization, would be included in an employer's mission statement.

Explanation and key takeaway: A mission statement is important for any company to have, whether it's been around for a hundred years or is just developing. The mission statement will allow others that don't know much about the business to understand the purpose and direction that the company wishes to go. A mission statement has three main parts. The first will show the core values that a company holds: What is most important for a company to maintain? The second part would be the goals that a company has: What do they wish to achieve throughout their lifetime? The third, and most important part, is a statement of the objective of the business. An HRM should know a company's mission statement inside and out, not only to be able to educate new employees, but to ensure that the business is also staying in line with their mission statement throughout all of their operations.

21. This refers to when an employee is prepared for future responsibility:

    A. Education

    B. Training

    C. Needs assessment

    D. Development

Answer - **D** - Development is when an employee is prepared for future responsibility.

Explanation and key takeaway: Training and Development are both crucial to the roles of an HRM, but the two are different from each other. Development refers to the preparation and learning an employee goes through when they have already been working for a business. They might undergo development in order to train for a new position, or just to improve the quality of their work. Development might include seminars, conventions, or presentations that can increase skill and knowledge. It might be recertification or the requirement of a higher degree in order to improve their overall knowledge. Training would refer to all of this, but before, or just after, hiring a new employee.

22. What does a mentor NOT do?

    A. Advise

    B. Mentor

    C. Reprimand

    D. Support

Answer - C - A mentor does not reprimand. A mentor offers advice, mentorship, and support.

Explanation and key takeaway: A

mentor might be given to a new employee in order to act as an advisor, counselor, or support them during the process of training, or in the initial months, as they get used to a position. The mentor would offer advice and feedback on their behavior, as well as give tips to ensure that they find success. A mentor is not to be seen as an authority figure, such as someone that would fire, punish, or reprimand the employee. They might suggest behavior modification or present information to an HRM, should the employee break a serious rule or commit a crime.

Part 5 – Employee and Labor Relations

Employee and Labor Relations is anything that is involved with the legal protection of worker's rights, among other categories related to unions and strikes. As an HRM, you might never work for a company that even allows labor unions. This might also be a specific area of work for some HRMs as well. No matter what the case is, it's incredibly important to be aware of worker's rights and everything that is in place to ensure they are receiving fair treatment.

1. If an employee ever decides that they no longer wish to be represented by their union, they must:

    A. Request for a decertification election

    B. Undergo an investigation by the NLRB

    C. Put in a two-weeks' notice

    D. None of the above

Answer - A - Request for a decertification election is what an employee must do if they ever decide that they no longer wish to be represented by their union.

Explanation and key takeaway: Sometimes, an employee might decide that they no longer wish to be represented by their union. If this is the case, they will have to undergo a decertification election. Before that can be done, there must be at least a 30 percent petition for the election, with signatures submitted 60-90 days before a contract is to end. When it comes time for a decertification election, the person that wishes to leave the union will have to receive a majority vote.

2. Which act prohibits employers with 15 or more workers from discriminating, whether it's in an employment, public service, transportation, public accommodations, or telecom position?

   A. The Labor Management Relations Act

   B. Wage Discrimination in Employment Act

   C. Title VII of the Civil Rights Act

D. Executive Order 11246

Answer - C - Title VII of the Civil Rights Act prohibits employers with 15 or more workers from discriminating, whether it's in an employment, public service, transportation, public accommodations, or telecom position.

> **Explanation and key takeaway:** Title VII of the Civil Rights Act states: "It shall be an unlawful employment practice for an employer ... to discriminate against any individual with respect to his compensation, terms, conditions, or privileges of employment, because of such individual's race, color, religion, sex, or national origin." This protects workers from discrimination that are in positions of employment involved in public service or public transportation, and other accommodations or telecom positions. No person can be discriminated against during hiring or firing, compensation, promotion, layoff, recall, recruitment, or pay. An HRM needs to be very aware of everything this act protects in order to ensure employees are treated fairly.

3. An agency shop:

   A. Is a firm that requires employers

to sign up with a union within the first week of employment

B. Is a firm that requires employees to pay union fees if they refuse to join the union

C. Is a firm that oversees the union shop

D. None of the above

Answer - B - A firm that requires employers to pay union fees if they refuse to join the union is known as an agency shop.

Explanation and key takeaway: There are many different types of unions that you might experience, either in an HRM or other employment position. Some unions require membership, others don't. It's important to be aware of all the different types of unions in order to ensure that all the proper rules and regulations are being followed. An agency shop is a union in which an employer could hire union or non-union workers. Upon employment, that new worker can either join the union or not. If they decide not to join, in an agency shop, they would have to pay a certain fee in order to cover the various collective bargaining costs.

4. The purpose of a grievance procedure in a union setting is:

   A. To give all complaints

   B. Conflict resolution

   C. Preparing funeral documents for employees

   D. Grievance counseling for family deaths

Answer - B - Conflict resolution is the purpose of a grievance procedure in a union setting.

Explanation and key takeaway: In a union setting, there might be times that disputes arise in which a settlement needs to be reached. In order to resolve conflict, a grievance procedure might be used in order to keep things professional and productive. The process starts with a written letter to an employer from the union member, in which the grievance would be outlined. This might deal with anything from monetary compensation to personal interactions. The grievance is unique and whatever the employee is experiencing.

After that, a meeting will occur in which the grievance will be discussed, and afterward, there will be a settlement.

5. Sometimes, employees are laid off even though it's not their fault whatsoever. Luckily, there is coverage for their missed wages, known as:

   A. The Shirley Act of 1992

   B. Medicare

   C. Unemployment compensation

   D. Worker's compensation

Answer - C - Unemployment compensation covers when employees are laid off even though it's not their fault whatsoever.

> **Explanation and key takeaway:** In some cases, an HRM might be involved in the layoff of different employees. This is an unfortunate time, but there is at least compensation to be given to employees that experience this layoff. This is referred to as unemployment compensation. This is usually calculated by taking the gross wages from two different quarters, halving that, and multiplying by .03. Unemployment does not pay as much as

normal compensation, and the terms will be different based on an employee's length with a company, ability to find more work, and how much they had to be made within the rest of the year. Sometimes, severance packages are given during layoffs, but these are not to be interchanged with unemployment compensation.

6. A union shop requires:

    A. Members to become part of the union within a specified time period

    B. The possibility of mandatory membership before hiring

    C. Nothing. Anyone can join or leave a union whenever they want

    D. Union fees, whether someone wants to be in the union or not

Answer - A – In a union shop, members are to become part of the union within a specified time period.

Explanation and key takeaway: Union shops are part of a security clause put in place with collective bargaining. By requiring that new employees are required to join a union, it ensures that the employers are doing their share of fair hiring. By giving a time limit on when union participation is required, it gives the employee a chance to make sure that they enjoy the position before agreeing to join a union. The NRLA requires a 30 day maximum from the date that employees are hired for them to decide if they wish to join the union shop. The employee that doesn't join the shop can then be fired after the agreed period of time. They might also be fired for failing to pay the required union fees, though the specifications vary depending on the agreement created when the employee was hired.

7. Which of these was enacted by Congress in 1935?

    A. National Labor Relations Act

    B. Title I of the Americans with Disabilities Act

    C. The Wagner Act

    D. A and C

Answer - **D** - The Wagner Act and The National Labor Relations Act are interchangeable terms for what was enacted by

Congress in 1935.

Explanation and key takeaway: A union shop might also be referred to as a post-entry closed shop, either on the test or in a professional setting. It is a form of union security in which those that are hired must join a union within a specified period of time. This enables employees to get a chance to know if they like the position before they decide to commit to that particular union. Every union can create their own specifications for the amount of time that someone has before they make their final decision.

8. Employees that are in a union are protected from termination and discrimination from their employer based on the fact that they are in a union with which of the following?

   A. An agency shop

   B. Section IV of the Vocational Rehabilitation Act

   C. The Labor Management Relations Act

   D. Equal Employment Opportunity Act

Answer - C - The Labor Management Relations Act protects employees that are in a union from termination and discrimination from their employer based on the fact that they are in a union.

Explanation and key takeaway: The Labor Management Relations Act might also be referred to as the Taft-Hartley Act. It stands to protect workers involved in unions as well as the right of workers to unionize. It explains that if workers are not given the opportunity to actively protect their individual and professional rights, then they could cause strikes that might upset the balance of production and commerce. It also goes on to ensure that employees in a union, versus those that are not, cannot be discriminated against because of their union status. It is important for HRMs to be aware of the importance of this act, in order to protect union worker's rights, and to be able to easily identify if something wrong is being done.

9. The _____ prohibits mandatory retirement based on an employee's age.

   A. Age Discrimination in Employment Act (1967)

B. Title IV of the Americans with Disabilities Act (1990)

C. Retirement Discrimination in Employment Act (1967)

D. Age Discrimination in Employment Act (1993)

Answer - B - Title IV of the Americans with Disabilities Act prohibits mandatory retirement based on an employee's age.

Explanation and key takeaway: The Americans with Disabilities Act is in place to protect anyone that might have a disability. Disabilities include hearing impairments, physical disabilities, and anything else that might give certain workers unfair disadvantages. In order to ensure these workers don't get discriminated against, the Americans with Disabilities Act covers everything that an employee needs to ensure they will not be discriminated against for any impairments they might have. This also covers pregnancy, as that is considered a short-term disability, should an employee become pregnant while working for a company.

10. Which is NOT a phase in labor relations?

   A. Extinction

   B. Collective bargaining

   C. Union organizing

   D. Contract administration

Answer - B - Extinction is not a phase in labor relations. Collective bargaining, union organizing, and contract administration are all phases in labor relations.

Explanation and key takeaway: There are three phases that are involved in labor relations. The first one is union organizing. This occurs when workers start to evaluate their own rights and needs, determining if there are steps they need to take in order to increase benefits and decrease inequalities. The second step would be collective bargaining, or negotiation of the agreements of labor. This might include different tactics and strategies to resolve conflict with the employer. The third phase is contract administration, which involves drafting legal agreements with employers to ensure that what was discussed is carried out through an agreement.

11. All of the following are types of strikes, except:

   A. Economic strike

   B. Wildcat strike

   C. Empathy strike

   D. None of these are types of strikes

Answer - C - An empathy strike is not a type of strike. Economic and Wildcat strikes both are.

Explanation and key takeaway: There are many different strikes that a union might start, and it's important to know the differences between them. An economic strike will happen if a union and employer fail to elicit a new contract that the union wanted in the first place. An unfair labor practice strike is one that would come about because the company has violated the NLRA. A wildcat strike is one that is unauthorized and usually spontaneous or unplanned. A sympathy strike is one that occurs in support of another strike that is occurring. Knowing all about the different types of strikes is important in order to understand the different rights and agreements that workers and employers have with each other.

12. One particular Act that addressed unfair labor union practices amended the NLRA. Which act did this?

  A. Landrum-Griffin Act

  B. Administration Act of 1995

  C. Taft-Hartley Act

  D. Fair Labor Act

Answer - C - The Taft-Hartley Act amended the NLRA and addressed unfair labor union practices.

Explanation and key takeaway: The Taft-Hartley Act might also be referred to as the Labor Management Relations Act. This was put in place in order to restrict certain powers that unions have. It also restricts certain activities, and makes it so that labor unions have to communicate with their employers about the different activities they plan to involve themselves in. This also requires union leaders to take on a non-communist oath, and made closed shops illegal.

While unions have many legal rights,

employers of different unions do as well, and they need to ensure that unions don't have too much strength, to the point where they can take advantage of their power in numbers. An HRM should know the differences, power balances, and what's allowed to occur between unions and employers, as well as any illegal activities that might go on within unions.

13. Which form of shop is illegal?

    A. Closed shop

    B. Union shop

    C. Agency shop

    D. Employment shop

Answer - A - A closed shop is illegal. Union, agency, and employment shops are all legal.

> **Explanation and key takeaway:** Closed shops were made illegal with the Taft-Hartley Act, in order to ensure that employers retained a certain amount of power and the activities of unions were limited. In response to the outlaw of closed shops, union shops became popular, which involve employees having to join a union within a certain amount of time. This gives

employers the chance to pick from a wider pool, while also ensuring that union workers have a say over who gets hired as well. Using a union shop versus a closed shop gives a more diverse pool for who might be accepted into the interview process.

14. "Salting" refers to:

    A. The act of taking positions that are empty due to a strike

    B. When a union organizer is working within a company that their union wants to unionize

    C. When a union organizer is working within a company that wishes to dismantle a union

    D. When a non-union employee supports the actions of the union of their company

Answer - B – When a union organizer is working within a company that their union wants to unionize, it is referred to as "salting."

Explanation and key takeaway: "Salting" is the process of a union laborer getting a position of employment with the intention of unionizing that job. A person who does this is referred to as a "salt." This is a legal strategy, even though in some workplace settings, the discussion of unions between members and non-members is illegal. If someone is caught "salting" in a new position, they might be legally fired for not showing genuine interest in a job. HRMs should be aware of this tactic, and look out for it in the hiring process. While not all "salters" have negative intentions, they might waste training hours and costs if they lie about the time that they plan to spend in a certain position.

15. At a local company, there is a security guard, a janitor, an electrician, and five other unskilled laborers. Which of these groups of workers would be the most likely to be in a unionized organization with their own bargaining unit?

    A. The janitor

    B. The unskilled laborers

    C. The security guard

    D. None of these would be in a union

Answer - C - The security guards is the most

likely to be in a unionized organization with their own bargaining unit.

Explanation and key takeaway: The types of workers most commonly in unions are laborers. These might include machinists, autoworkers, electrical workers, or other positions of general labor. However, the type of job that can be unionized is not limited to these roles.

These unions might have their own bargaining unit as well. A bargaining unit is a selected group of workers that might be the voice of the rest of the workers. They work closely together in a community of shared interests, in order to represent the labor union. Knowing the different types of bargaining units and unionized organizations is important, and knowing specific names and titles is helpful as well, both on the test and in a professional setting.

16. In order to hold an election, ____ percent of employees have to sign union representation cards.

    A. 50

    B. 25

C. 70

D. 30

Answer - D - 30 percent of employees have to sign union representation cards in order to hold an election.

Explanation and key takeaway: Each union creates their own terms and representative resolutions, but there are certain factors that all union officers and HRMs should know when it comes time for a union election. Once an election occurs, there are many different things that might happen, but before it can even begin, the union workers must show interest. A need for an election must be presented, and at least 30 percent of union workers have to agree to this election for it to take place.

17. A strike that is unapproved by a union is known as a _____

   A. Lockout

   B. Secondary strike

   C. Wildcat strike

   D. Economic strike

Answer - C - A wildcat strike is one that is

unapproved by a union. A lockout, secondary, and economic strike are all types of strikes that have been approved by a union before taking place.

Explanation and key takeaway: Before striking, there must be an agreement among the leaders of a union. This is to ensure that this is the proper action to take. Sometimes, a strike might cause more harm than good, so it's important to make sure that striking is going to elicit a productive change, rather than just be the reaction of some heated emotions. A wildcat strike occurs when there is not any approval from the leadership of a union. A wildcat strike might also be known as an unofficial industrial action.

18. A Third-party determination would be involved in which step of the grievance procedure?

   A. This is the first thing done

   B. It's done whenever it's convenient

   C. This is done in the final step

   D. This is not needed in a grievance procedure

Answer - C - The final step of a grievance procedure involves a third-party determination.

Explanation and key takeaway: The point of a grievance procedure is to hopefully resolve a conflict that has arisen. Sometimes, this might mean drafting up a new contract, or increasing a certain wage. There are different reasons why a grievance procedure might occur, but many of the steps will be similar once one is decided upon. If no resolution is met, then a third-party determination might come in handy. A third-party determination is when someone else comes in to help find a resolution, and they might even do some speaking or discussing on behalf of one of the members involved in a grievance procedure.

19. When a strike has been threatened, what is management the most interested in?

    A. How much money is going to be lost

    B. Which employees thought of the strike first

    C. Getting media and police

involved

D. Maintaining service and production of the company

Answer - D - Maintaining service and production of a particular company is what management is most interested in when a strike has been threatened.

Explanation and key takeaway: When a strike has been threatened, it can cause serious tension in the workplace. Most of the time, a strike is a final resort. Usually, there can be steps taken before a union goes through with a strike. In the chance that it still occurs, an HRM needs to be prepared for what to do next. Their main concern is going to regard how service will be maintained, as well as any necessary production of the company: Will services need to be halted, or can another department take on these duties?

Of course, the media might get involved, but this shouldn't be the concern of the HRM. There might be money lost and supplies wasted as well, but this would be the concern for someone other than the HRM. It takes an entire union to organize and carry out a strike, so it can not be blamed on one person either, and if it is, that is in a violation of the very Act that stands in place to protect union workers.

20. Which of these laws deals with collective bargaining among federal employees?

    A. Federal Labor Relations Act

    B. Civil Service Reform Act

    C. Labor-Management Relations Act

    D. National Labor Protection Act

Answer - B - The Civil Service Reform Act deals with collective bargaining among federal employees.

Explanation and key takeaway: Collective bargaining is the act of negotiation of wages or other employee conditions, specifically carried out by an organized group that was typically chosen to serve as representatives for the thoughts and feelings of the majority. Collective bargaining might typically be done by the union leaders, or by one representative that was elected to be the voice for concern. The Civil Service Reform Act of 1978 protects the rights of workers to organize collective bargaining unions, ensuring that all workers are allowed to fight for their rights without fear of reprimand.

Part 6 – Risk Management

Risk Management is going to be a big part of the test as well. It regards anything that involves the safety and protection of different employees. Sometimes, a company might have risk management programs that aren't useful, take up costs, and hold the company back. Other times, there might be risk management procedures that actually don't protect workers enough. No one should have to fear for their safety in a position that doesn't have to be dangerous, so it's crucial for HRMs to make sure they know as much as possible, to ensure that their workers are protected and free from harm.

1. The Drug-Free Workplace Act:

   A. Creates regulations for how employers inform employees of what drug use might be a violation.

   B. Does not consider tobacco and alcohol-controlled substances

   C. Only applies to those employers that have contracts or grants with the government.

D. All of the above

Answer - D - The Drug-Free Workplace Act is in place to inform employees of the requirements, what might be a violation, spreading awareness, and training supervisors. It does not consider tobacco and alcohol as controlled substances, and it only applies to those employers that have contracts or grants with the government.

> **Explanation and key takeaway:** One thing an HRM might often run into is drug use within the workplace. Some companies might fall under the Drug-Free Workplace Act of 1988, in which the company receives a specific grant to ensure that they create a drug-free work zone. This might involve issuing drug tests and doing extensive background checks on employees to ensure that no drug abuse is taking place. Those companies that are given grants because of the Drug-Free Workplace act must inform employees of certain dangers or violations that should occur if drug use is detected. Not all HRMs will work for a company that falls under the Drug-Free Workplace Act, but it is still important to be aware of this Act in order to pass the test.

2. Which of the following areas of study is used for addressing physical demands experienced by people within a business?

   A. Ergonomics

   B. Comfort settings

   C. Physical zoning

   D. None of the above

Answer - **A** - Ergonomics is a work environment study that is used for addressing physical demands experienced by people within a business.

Explanation and key takeaway: Ergonomics is the study of how people work efficiently within the environment they are employed. An HRM will have extensive knowledge of ergonomics, and the practices and studies that come along with the various theories involved with how an employee interacts with their environment. Ergonomics aims to refine products, tools, and services that help make people's jobs much easier. Ergonomics might involve designing a more efficient desk or computer chair, or it might be more extensive, such as developing the method in which a company does its hiring.

3. OSHA uses this form to record illnesses, accidents, and injuries:

   A. OSHA notification report

   B. Form 20

   C. Form 2000

   D. Form 200

Answer - D - Form 200 is used by OSHA to record illnesses, accidents, and injuries.

Explanation and key takeaway: The Occupational Safety and Health Administration sets standards for employees in terms of safety and health. They are the administration that is in charge of ensuring employees are taken care of, and that if an injury does occur, it is handled properly. There are many different interactions an HRM might have with someone from OSHA, so the more aware they are of what is going on within the operations of OSHA, the better they will be able to resolve an issue, should one arise. The dealings with OSHA, such as what forms or procedures need to be dealt with, is important in order to ensure the proper recordings are made. For example, OSHA uses something known as a Form 200 to record illnesses, accidents, and injuries. That term alone might be something often discussed within a company and with specific HRMs and their employees.

4. What are the three approaches to effective safety management?

    A. Human resources, engineering, and organizational

    B. Organizational, human resources, and individual

    C. Individual, engineering, and human resources

    D. Organizational, engineering, and individual

Answer - D - Organizational, engineering, and individual are the three approaches to effective safety management. Human resources is not considered one of them and is instead representative of the collection of all three.

Explanation and key takeaway: There are many different procedures a company can choose to use within their safety department to protect workers. There are some key approaches that should be known by all HRMs for how different safety management will be effectively used. One is an organizational approach: What is occurring within an organization that provides safety, and what organizational factors need to be improved upon in order to ensure safety measurements are being reached? Another approach is engineering: Are certain machines safe, and are there processes for using machines that are in place to make sure all workers are protected? Another approach is individual: Are the employees safe on an individual level, and can those around an employee feel safe among their fellow workers?

5. The order in which actions should be taken in order to eliminate work-safety problems is referred to as:

   A. Safety studies

   B. Time and motion progression

   C. Safety hierarchy

   D. Motion timeline

Answer - C - Safety hierarchy refers to the

order in which actions should be taken in order to eliminate work-safety problems.

Explanation and key takeaway: A safety hierarchy can refer to the processes of risk control. There are a certain number of actions that need to be taken in order to make sure work-safety problems are eliminated. The first step is to identify anything that might be hazardous or dangerous. An HRM has to look around a workplace and the environment that workers will be subjected to, and identify each and every hazard that might cause an employee potential harm. The second would be risk identification: Is there a risk or chance that something might happen? After that, risk assessment and risk control follow to ensure all of these problems are properly dealt with, or that there is at least a plan in place to help if something does happen to go wrong. The final two steps of the hierarchy involve documenting and monitoring the process and the continued process of keeping everything safe and hazard-free.

6. The Occupational Safety and Health Act defines which of these as an injury or illness?

A. Minor injuries

B. Injury and illness related deaths

C. Disability injuries

D. All of the above

Answer - D - Disability injuries, injury and illness related deaths, and minor injuries are all defined as an injury or illness by the Occupational Safety and Health Act.

Explanation and key takeaway: According to the United States Department of Labor, the Occupational Safety and Health Act exists, "To assure safe and healthful working conditions for working men and women; by authorizing enforcement of the standards developed under the Act; by assisting and encouraging the States in their efforts to assure safe and healthful working conditions; by providing for research, information, education, and training in the field of occupational safety and health; and for other purposes."

7. One of the biggest causes of stress in a workplace environment includes:

A. Gaining popularity among

coworkers

B. Knowing when break-time is

C. Having little personal control in a job

D. Outside factors the employee brings in

Answer - C - Having little personal control in a job is one of the biggest causes of stress in a workplace environment.

> **Explanation and key takeaway:** In order to properly assess what might cause an employee to behave a certain way, it is important to look at everything that might elicit stress, or figure out any cause of emotional anxiety that could affect their work habits. One of the biggest causes of stress in a workplace is when an employee feels as though they don't have much personal control. This can cause them to feel as though they are falling behind, and they might not perform as well if they don't have the confidence it takes to know that they can take charge.

8. If an employer must conduct an accident investigation, when it comes to completing reports, they must make

sure to:

A. Talk to the person that was injured, as well as the witness

B. Make sure the company's safety is put first

C. Only fill out a report if there was a death involved

D. Convince the employee not to make any reports on the accident

Answer - A – An employer must talk to the person that was injured, as well as a witness, when they want to conduct an accident investigation and properly fill out the reports.

Explanation and key takeaway: Some companies may never have to worry about having an accident or causing one of their employees' harm. Unfortunately, there are plenty of work environments that are prone to accidents, but steps can be taken to prevent and resolve workplace accidents. One of the first steps for starting an accident investigation is to isolate the accident scene. This step is important in making sure that no one else can end up getting hurt in the same way. It is also important to make sure that the scene can't be altered in a situation that might destroy evidence. The injured worker should also be removed immediately, of course, in order to receive proper treatment. The next step is to record any evidence to ensure that it was a complete accident and not something intentional, or something caused by negligence. After the scene has been assessed, it is time to identify witnesses and speak to the employee that was injured, as long as they are healthy enough and in a state where they can recall what happened.

9. Which of the below describes a recordable case:

   A. An accident in which an employee received a minor cut

   B. An incident involves any and all forms of medical treatment

   C. An incident when the employee felt even a small instance of physical or emotional pain, related to the job or not

   D. An injury or death occurred

Answer - D - If an injury or death has occurred, this is considered a recordable case.

Explanation and key takeaway: Some injuries or accidents don't always need to be recorded if they are not very serious. OSHA has certain standards that layout whether or not an injury is recordable or needing to be recorded. If it is an injury that cannot be treated with first aid, such as a minor cut, bump, or burn, then it must be recorded. Anytime an employee has to spend days away from work because of the accident, or seek professional medical treatment, they need to record their injury. If there is a loss of consciousness, or even worse, death, this is certainly something that needs to be recorded. If it is an injury that is not work-related, it does not need to be recorded by OSHA.

10. In which of the following situations might a polygraph test be administered?

    A. An employee calls off sick without a doctor's note

    B. When hiring a guard or member of a security firm that would be responsible for, or have access to, a controlled substance

    C. When company property exceeding $500 goes missing

D. Technically, whenever an employer wants

Answer - B - When hiring a guard or member of a security firm that would be responsible for, or have access to, a controlled substance is an instance in which a polygraph test might be administered.

> **Explanation and key takeaway:** Employers are not allowed to give polygraph tests whenever they want, or when an employee calls off sick without a doctor's note. If more than $500 worth of company property goes missing, a police investigation might follow, in which, in rare circumstances, a polygraph test would be administered. Most of the time, however, polygraphs are only given when it is important to protect some aspect of security in a job. Whether an employee is working with classified information or substances that can cause destruction and harm, a polygraph test will likely be administered, but mostly, at the discretion of the HRM or someone in a higher position. Sometimes, if the employee refuses to take a polygraph test, they might not qualify for that position.

11. An MSDS would be required when:

A. A hazardous chemical is processed, stored, or used

B. An employee that might be dealing with hazardous materials is hired

C. A hazardous material goes missing

D. A hazardous material explodes

Answer - A - When a hazardous chemical is processed, stored, or used, an MSDS would be required.

Explanation and key takeaway: A Material Safety Data Sheet (MSDS) is required when there is any handling of a hazardous chemical. Whether this chemical is processed, stored, or used, an MSDS is required in order to make sure that the activity is properly monitored. They might be placed directly in the workplace, or right where certain hazardous materials are kept and stored. They are reminders to those around that there is a hazardous material and certain safety precautions need to be used in order to make sure that no harm can come to the employees involved with the hazardous material. This also protects employers, as they give employees the responsibility of properly dealing with these chemicals and materials.

12. Which of the following is NOT a wellness program?

   A. Smoking cessation

   B. Child-care education

   C. Cancer prevention education

   D. YMCA membership

Answer - D - A YMCA membership would not be considered a wellness program. Smoking cessation, child-care education, or cancer prevention education could be considered wellness programs depending on company policy.

Explanation and key takeaway: Those in charge of running a company or certain business might want to include some employee wellness programs to ensure that their staff is healthy and happy. These are programs paid for by the employers and are not things that can be traded for cash or liquefied. For example, an employer might want to hold a cancer prevention meeting in which a professional discusses ways in which employees can prevent themselves from getting cancer. By having educated employees, the employers can be certain that they are doing their best to have workers that will live long and stay productive. An onsite fitness center and the availability of different types of snacks would also be considered types of employee wellness programs.

13. Machine guarding is:

    A. Standards that include general requirements for machinery to be protected, in order to ensure it doesn't cause any hazard to employees or the operator

    B. The act of guarding a machine

    C. A training program required by anyone that will come in contact with a hazardous machine within their first 30 days of employment

    D. All of the above

Answer - A - Standards that include general requirements for machinery to be protected, in order to ensure it doesn't cause any hazard to employees or the operator is known as machine guarding. The act of guarding a machine, or a training program required by anyone that will come in contact with a hazardous machine within their first 30 days of employment would have different terms.

Explanation and key takeaway: Machine guarding involves different rules as well as various physical materials that protect employees from dangerous machines. These standards weren't always in place, but by requiring that certain machines have certain protecting guards, the employees that are around that machine avoid any possibility of danger. Any machine that might have flying chips, rotating parts, or sparks might require machine guarding. This will usually be very brightly colored in order remind those around that dangerous parts exist underneath.

14. What is the leading cause of workplace death?

    A. Getting struck by an object

    B. Electrocution

    C. Fatal falling

    D. Getting caught in-between objects

Answer - C – Fatal falling is the leading cause of death in the workplace. The other three options - electrocution, getting struck by an object, and getting caught in-between objects - are the next three most common causes of death.

> **Explanation and key takeaway:** The leading causes of workplace deaths are involved with the construction industry. The Fatal Four is a term coined by OSHA that describes the top four causes of death in the construction industry. The first is fatal falling, which accounts for over a third of construction deaths. The following three are electrocution, getting struck by an object, and getting caught in between objects.

15. When was the Occupational Safety and Health Act passed?

    A. 1989

    B. 1970

    C. 1969

    D. 1972

Answer - B - 1970 is when the Occupational Safety and Health Act was passed.

Explanation and key takeaway: At one point in history, it was cheaper to replace dead or injured workers rather than put safety regulations in place that protected against further deaths and injuries. In order to maintain worker morale, the Occupational Safety and Health Act was passed in 1970 to ensure that companies were doing everything they could to ensure no injury or death occurred that could have been easily prevented. It is important to remember these years in order to realize just how recently workers went without some of these basic rights and protections. It is also important for HRMs to understand the history of workplace safety in order to prevent it from happening again. While some specific years can be challenging to remember, these precise bits of information are needed to ensure passing the test.

16. Safety is best described with which option?

    A. The staff are involved in making sure no accidents happen

    B. The staff are hired to protect other staff members

C. When the physical well being of any person is protected

D. The measurements and precautions in place to ensure that no one gets harmed

Answer - C - When the physical well being of any person is protected, it is known as safety.

Explanation and key takeaway: The overall definition of safety is the condition of protection. When one person can be certain that everything is in place to ensure that they can't get hurt, they will perform much better. It is a natural human instinct to want to feel safe. It is in our biology, so of course, when workers feel like they are safe and protected, they will be able to perform much better than if they were in any other situation.

Part 7 – Learning and Development

Learning and Development covers how an HRM is looking at their company and figuring out what needs to be done to make sure that it continually develops positively. An HRM will analyze different aspects of a job to make sure there is less turnover, more employee satisfaction, and a profit margin that makes a business grow over time, rather than remain stagnant. This wasn't always a large part of the test, but it has certainly become an important set of questions an HRM to know.

1. A reduction in errors and turnover are just some of the benefits of:

    A. Hiring

    B. Staffing

    C. Planning

    D. Training

Answer - D - Training has benefits that include a reduction in errors and employee turnover.

Explanation and key takeaway: Training is important for obvious reasons, including the need to make sure that workers know what they're doing within a certain company. It is also important for a business in an individual sense, as it allows for the business to receive certain benefits as well. If there is an overall reduction of errors, then that means less money will be wasted and fewer resources will be used in order to retrain employees, or to get the risk management involved to resolve an issue. There is also less employee turnover.

During training, the employee gets the chance to really see what working in that position is like, so if they don't like what it involves, they can leave before they become too committed. It also gives them the chance to get comfortable, so they can find it easier to adjust to the certain lifestyles that a job might include. These are just a few of the benefits of training that should be known by an HRM in order to pass the test.

2. A cause and effect diagram can also be described as:

A. A bell curve

B. Ishikawa diagram

C. Clerical graph

D. Pareto analysis

Answer - B - An Ishikawa diagram can also be described as a cause and effect diagram.

Explanation and key takeaway: An Ishikawa diagram is one that was created by Kaoru Ishikawa. All types of Ishikawa diagrams show the causes that a specific event might have. A herringbone, Fishikawa, fishbone diagram, or cause-and-effect diagram are all interchangeable terms and are known as Ishikawa diagrams. Ishikawa diagrams force those that create the diagram to really look at all the causes of a certain problem. By doing this, an HRM might find a problem causer that they didn't expect, perhaps in a small department they weren't giving attention to. By looking at more obvious causes and effects, you might miss out on the small things that are really causing serious damage in a certain industry.

3. Taking the number of terminations,

times 100, and dividing it by the average number of employees allows you to calculate:

A. Hiring capacity

B. How many employees you can fire in the next year

C. Turnover rates

D. The number of exemptions you can add

Answer - C - Turnover rates can be calculated by taking the number of terminations, times 100, and dividing it by the average number of employees.

Explanation and key takeaway: Turnover, in terms of employment, refers to the act of using a new employee as a replacement for the old. Turnover looks at the number of employees that enter and exit a particular company and the rate at which this happens. Certain positions might have a high turnover, like in a fast food restaurant or a retailer. Other positions might not have any turnover at all, maintaining the same employees for years at a time. Some positions, like seasonal jobs, might not be affected by turnover as much as others. There are many businesses, however, that might suffer greatly from high turnover rates. Recruiting, interviewing, and training all take time and money from a business, so if this has to happen regularly, resources might not be as high as they could be. In order to ensure there isn't a problem with the company, an HRM should track turnover rates. This can be done with this formula: (Number of terminations)(100) / (average number of employees).

4. If an employer wants to drug test their candidates, which of the following is true?

    A. They have to test every single person they hire

    B. They can choose who they want to drug test

    C. Drug tests must be completed with blood and urine

    D. A and C

Answer - B - Employers can choose who they want to drug test. If drug tests are chosen, they can be conducted in whichever way the employee prefers, including taking blood, urine, or hair samples. Employers don't have to drug test everyone they hire, though they do have to stay consistent with the group they choose to test.

Explanation and key takeaway: Employers have the right to decide if they want to drug test their candidates or not, but if they choose to do so, they have to ensure that they are being fair with those they pick to test. Only choosing to test a certain candidate is not fair and can be an act of discrimination. However, only choosing to test employees with more important duties than those with other positions is a common practice. For instance, at a hotel, those that are in high managerial positions might have to be drug tested, but maids or concierge staff don't have as many responsibilities, so employers might save money by choosing not to test this specific category of workers. In order to ensure there is no discrimination taking place, employers have to make sure they're maintaining consistency with who is being tested.

5. The Pregnancy Discrimination Act of 1978 states that employers should consider pregnancy a:

A. Short-term disability

B. Long-term disability

C. Injury

D. Pregnancy should not be treated any differently

Answer - A – Pregnancy is treated as a short-term disability, according to The Pregnancy Discrimination Act of 1978.

Explanation and key takeaway: The Pregnancy Discrimination Act of 1978 states, "The terms 'because of sex' or 'on the basis of sex' include, but are not limited to, because of or on the basis of pregnancy, childbirth, or related medical conditions; and women affected by pregnancy, childbirth, or related medical conditions shall be treated the same for all employment-related purposes, including receipt of benefits under fringe benefit programs, as other persons not so affected but similar in their ability or inability to work." This protects employees that are pregnant, or choose to become pregnant, from discrimination. In order to go through the proper paperwork, HRMs are encouraged to treat a pregnancy as a

short-term disability, meaning that the
employee will be back to work after a
period of time has been taken off.

6. Affirmative action gives demographic
information that provides a:

   A. Organizational availability

   B. Determination of availability

   C. Job group profile

   D. Organizational analysis

Answer - B - Determination of availability can
be found through the demographic information
provided by affirmative action.

Explanation and key takeaway:
Affirmative action is a policy that aims to
protect certain groups that commonly
experience discrimination, by ensuring that
fair opportunity is given to minorities that
might otherwise be overlooked,
intentionally or unintentionally.
Sometimes, there might not be as high of a
demographic of protected groups in one
area as there is another, so there can't be
set standards for the number of employees
from protected groups that should be
hired. Instead, a determination of

availability should be explored in order to figure out what percentage of a protected group should be represented within a specific organization.

7. An HR manager that uses temporary workers during a certain season would use which type of contract with the temp agency?

    A. Third-party contract

    B. Temporary contract

    C. Organizational contract

    D. Brief contract

Answer - A - A third-party contract would be used if an HR manager decides to use temporary employment for their business with a temp agency.

Explanation and key takeaway: In some cases, temporary workers might need to be hired, either to replace an employee that is leaving, or due to a need for a higher workforce, perhaps in busy seasons. In order to protect the company and these temporary workers, an HRM might use a third-party contract in order to lay out the terms of the specific agreement between the agency and the company. The third-party contract would include how much time the employee is expected to work and the compensation that will be given for that short period of employment. These contracts might include different terms from what regular consistent employees are receiving as well.

8. The most important positions in a company are determined with:

   A. A job group profile

   B. Point factor method

   C. Employee training

   D. Operative analysis

Answer - B - A point factor method can help determine the most important positions in a company.

Explanation and key takeaway: During a job analysis, an HRM might need to determine what the most important position in a company might be. In order to do this, they might use a point factor method. This would first involve selecting a job cluster of the company. From there, the HRM would pick out factors of each of those jobs and determine a degree or scale of what makes these compensable. Different weights would be given to different aspects, and from there, a score can be added to determine which positions hold the most value. This is always important to do to ensure that fair labor is being given, as well as fair compensation. Doing this once doesn't mean that it doesn't need to be done again. It should be something included annually, if not more.

9. An EEO survey must be completed annually by:

   A. A library

   B. A federal subcontractor

   C. A bank that issues U.S. savings bonds

   D. A small local government

Answer - C - A bank that issues U.S. savings bonds must complete an annual EEO survey.

   Explanation and key takeaway: An equal employment opportunity survey is one that might be required of various institutions on a regular basis. For example, a bank that issues U.S. savings bonds might be required to fill one out annually. This survey will help determine the different demographics of the business, including what race, ethnicity, and gender is present in a certain work environment, ensuring there is equality among employees and the various positions. By implementing this survey in different positions, employees can be sure that they will be protected from discrimination, and the public that might be involved with these positions can also be certain that there will be a diverse workforce that won't discriminate against them either.

10. What differentiates a goal and a strategy?

  A. A goal cannot exist without a strategy

  B. A goal is the end and a strategy is how you get there

  C. There is no difference

  D. Goals don't help achieve much and strategies are more important

Answer - B - A goal is the end and a strategy is how you get there.

Explanation and key takeaway – Every company needs to make sure that they are setting different goals, both at a corporate and an individual level. These goals might not always be met, but they are important to determine what needs to happen within an organization to meet these particular goals. This might include doubling profits from the year before, or sometimes even just trying to hire a more diverse set of employees. Before anything else can happen, a goal must be set. Once there is a goal in mind, a strategy needs to be created in order to achieve that goal. A strategy cannot exist without a goal in mind, or at least an idea of what one might want to achieve with their specified strategy.

11. Which would NOT be involved in a training needs analysis?

> A. Deciding if employees are getting paid too much
>
> B. Looking at the history of training
>
> C. Determining the required skills of a job
>
> D. analyses of the laws and procedures used on a job

Answer - A - Deciding if employees are getting paid too much would not be part of a training needs analysis. Looking at the history of training, determining the required skills of a job, and performing an analysis of the laws and procedures used on a job might all be included in a training needs analysis.

> **Explanation and key takeaway** – A training needs analysis, in terms of HR management, is an assessment of the needs required for training in a certain organization. Employees need to be skilled in their positions while making sure that they have the resources necessary for training as well. A training needs analysis looks at the previous, current, and future techniques of training that work, while trying to cut out any educational processes that aren't successful. Types of training needs analyses might include organizational, which looks at the needs of a business and their goals and strategies. A person analysis would look at the individuals being used in certain operational processes, determining if these people are knowledgeable in their positions. A work analysis, which might also be known as a task analysis, aims to

evaluate the specific tasks that are being performed. When these duties are analyzed, so can the effort that needs to go into training for these duties. A content analysis will look more at the laws and procedures used in a certain position. A training suitability analysis will look most specifically at training processes, determining if they are the right choice for the specific situation.

Part 8 – Talent Planning and Acquisition

Talent Planning and Acquisition is another part of the test that hasn't been as important in previous years. But with other operations like OSHA, and different laws that automatically protect workers, an HRM can be more focused now than ever on how to make sure their employees are well-trained and satisfied in a position. This includes making sure that before an employee goes through training; they are properly selected and fairly hired.

1. What is used to measure an employee's adherence to the performance standards put in place?

    A. Participative management

    B. Performance appraisal

    C. Lack of quality problems

    D. Concurrent validity

Answer - B - Performance appraisal is used to measure an employee's adherence to the performance standards put in place.

Explanation and key takeaway: A performance appraisal gives an employer the chance to address the issue of an employee failing to adhere to the performance standards. This appraisal might happen yearly, monthly, or not at all, depending on the company. An appraisal has no legal definitions, and what might be involved is different among various institutions. It might be done with a direct supervisor, or it could occur with an entire group of the heads of the department. It's important for an HRM to be aware of the various things that might be discussed within a performance appraisal, so they can ensure they're being fairly and properly conducted.

2. A third country national is someone that:

   A. Is a citizen of one country but works in two others

   B. Is a citizen of one country but has positions in more than one country at a time

   C. Is a citizen of one country that

works in a second but is employed by an organization that is headquartered in a third country

D. Someone that was brought from a third world country to work for a company

Answer - C - A citizen of one country that works in a second but is also employed by an organization that is headquartered in a third country is a third country national.

Explanation and key takeaway: It can be hard for those traveling with various visas to keep up with all the rules and regulations of a country, but HRMs need to be very aware of them all in order to protect the rights of their worker as well as the company from any illegal hiring. For instance, an HRM should be aware of the definition of a third country national, a person that might be applying for a visa in a country that isn't their country of origin, but only doing so to go to a different country in order to work. These definitions and restrictions can be confusing for some to remember, so it's important to not just memorize the specifications, but also be aware of why they're there in the first place.

3. The Family and Medical Leave Act allows employees to:

   A. Take up to 12 weeks of unpaid leave during a 6-month period

   B. Take up to 12 weeks of unpaid leave during a 12-month period

   C. Take up to 10 weeks unpaid leave during a 24-month period

   D. Take as much time as needed for a family medical emergency

Answer - B - Up to 12 weeks of unpaid leave can be taken during a 12-month period, according to The Family and Medical Leave Act, though there are standards that change the time period, depending on the situation.

Explanation and key takeaway: The Family and Medical Leave Act (FMLA) protects a worker's right to take family and medical leave if they need to. They are given 12 weeks within a 12-month period. This might include taking time off for the birth of a child, as well as leave to care for the child, including if a child is adopted.

4. If an employee's spouse is an active servicemember that becomes injured,

would this be covered by FMLA?

A. Yes, they would get 12 weeks of unpaid leave during a 12-month period

B. No, caring for servicemembers is exempt from FMLA

C. Yes, they would get 26 weeks of unpaid leave during a 12-month period

D. Yes, they would get 6 additional weeks of unpaid leave during a 2-month period

Answer - B - If an employee's spouse is an active servicemember that becomes injured, they would get 26 weeks of unpaid leave during a 12-month period.

Explanation and key takeaway: If an employee has a spouse, child, or another close family member with a serious health condition, they might be eligible to take FMLA leave in order to care for them. If the employee themselves has a serious health condition that keeps them from properly performing their job, they would also apply for FLMA. Twenty-six workweeks can also be taken during a 12-month period in order to care for a servicemember that has a serious illness or injury, and requires the care of their family member or spouse.

5. Affirmative Action:

   A. Is just a suggestion for how someone should go about their hiring processes, but not a requirement

   B. Does no good to help diversity in a company

   C. Allows HR managers to find imbalances among their workforce so they can remedy the underrepresentation of protected groups

   D. Allows different companies to receive tax breaks if they hire more convicted felons

Answer - C - HR managers can find imbalances among their workforce, so they can remedy the underrepresentation of protected groups, with affirmative action.

Explanation and key takeaway: Affirmative action calls on the knowledge of the HRMs to ensure that there is a fair representation within a certain workforce. This is done to make sure that there are no discriminatory practices in place and that everyone has an equal opportunity to get hired for the position.

6. When creating a job description, the ADA states that essential job functions need to be listed:

    A. If the employer wants

    B. With the most important duty first

    C. However the employer wishes

    D. With the most dangerous position listed first

Answer - B - The most important duty should be listed first in a job description, according to the ADA.

Explanation and key takeaway: The Americans with Disabilities Act states that when listing a job description, the most important duty should be listed first in order to give applicants a clear idea of the expectations that might be required of them should they end up in that specific position.

7. The Fair Labor Standards Act protects:

A. Minimum wage regulation

B. Children's work hours

C. Overtime Pay

D. All of the above

Answer - D - Overtime pay, children's work hours, and minimum wage regulation are all protected under The Fair Labor Standards Act.

Explanation and key takeaway: The Fair Labor Standards Act is one of the most important acts for HRMs to be aware of in order to ensure that their employees' most basic rights are being met within a corporation. This includes adhering to a federal minimum wage that must be met, with very few exceptions in place. This also makes sure records are being properly kept in order to ensure that the rights of employees are being protected. The FLSA is also responsible for establishing child labor standards and restricted hours for children of a certain age. Though there are more important factors within this act, these are the most basic to understand and remember.

8. When training programs are created, who has the copyright?

    A. The person being trained

    B. The CEO of a company

    C. The employer of the trainer that created the training program

    D. No one owns any training programs

Answer - C - The employer of the trainer that created the training program owns the copyright.

> **Explanation and key takeaway:** Even though an employee might think of a certain training program or way to teach skills and knowledge to new employees, the employer of the trainer is the one that still owns the copyright to any training program that is created. This is important to know in case a trainer moves to a different company and uses the same effective training methods in a competitive scenario.

9. When developing hiring plans, it's important to:

    A. Use a polygraph test on anyone

that seems suspicious

B. Check all references

C. Require blood testing

D. Use psychological methods for evaluating an employee

Answer - B - Checking all references is important when developing hiring plans.

Explanation and key takeaway: Checking references is a way that HRMs can be sure they are hiring the right employee. There are certain guidelines that need to be considered when checking references, however. Some companies have rules and regulations that state their employees aren't allowed to give any past information on a particular worker other than their last name and the dates in which they were employed. This protects workers that are no longer in a company from receiving biased feedback that could be false or misinform future potential managers.

10. What makes up a good MBO?

A. Measurable goals

B. Goals that are set much higher than something obtainable

C. Goals created by the supervisors

D. No goals at all- it's up to the employee to figure out what they want to achieve

Answer - A - Measurable goals make up a good MBO

Explanation and key takeaway: MBO stands for management by objectives. This is a six-step process that is used to integrate managerial activities to improve employee efficiency, as well as achieve corporate goals. The first step of an MBO is to define organizational goals. This starts with creating goals that are measurable and not ones that are too high to obtain. After that, individual employee objectives should be defined in order to determine what is needed on both a corporate and an individual level. There should be a continual monitor of progress, with a performance evaluation and feedback to follow. The last step would be a performance appraisal, and the then MBO can start over again.

11. If a potential employee might pose a security risk to the company, what is the best way to ensure they are the right hire?

   A. A polygraph test

   B. Drug testing

   C. Background check without permission

   D. Background check with permission

Answer - D - A background check with the employee's permission can be done if a potential candidate might pose a security risk to a certain company.

Explanation and key takeaway: Background checks can be given in order to ensure that the safety of other employees, as well as any customers that might engage with a business, aren't threatened. The important thing to remember with background checks, however, is that they must be given consistently. If an employer only gives background checks to people from certain neighborhoods, then they might be displaying forms of discrimination.

12. Which would NOT be considered external recruiting?

   A. Recruiting at schools

   B. Using media sources

   C. Promotion

   D. Using the help of an employment agency

Answer - C - Promotion would not be considered external recruiting.

Explanation and key takeaway: External recruiting refers to assessing outside candidates for a certain position rather than looking at the existing staff. This might be done by visiting schools where potential future candidates are about to graduate. Some companies find that hiring those with less experience will require a lower salary. Using media sources to gauge what is available might also be a form of external recruiting. An employment agency might also be used for external recruiting in order to seek out more qualified candidates that have been carefully selected by different professionals.

13. In the hiring process, if an employee gets asked about their past behavior, it would be considered a:

A. Directive

B. Stress

C. Behavioral interview

D. Non-directive

Answer - C - A behavioral interview is one that takes place in the hiring process when an employee gets asked about their past behavior.

Explanation and key takeaway: A behavioral interview is probably one of the most common types of interviews that employers use to get to know different candidates. In a behavioral job interview, candidates will be asked about how they might have reacted in previous situations that aren't even related to the workforce. This is to gauge what they might be like in different situations.

Conclusion

When the day of the test arrives, it's important to be prepared, relaxed, and focused. Even though it might be tempting to stay up late and cram as much studying in as possible, make sure that you rest properly before going in to take the test. Sometimes, studying last minute can actually clog up your brain and confuse your memory, so it's best to make sure you get some peaceful relaxation in beforehand.

While practicing this test multiple times can help, it's important that the concepts and ideas are understood rather than just memorized. None of these questions are going to be word-for-word on the actual exam, and are instead just created to mimic what previous tests might have included. The tests are always changing, so at the end of the day, it's not the answers that are important to know, but what the answers actually mean, and why they are the correct choices.

These are not the exact questions that will be on the test, only examples of the information that might be presented. In some years, there has even been more of an emphasis on certain sections than others. The tests are always changing to ensure that they don't become easier if a person has to take it more than once. There are also plenty of applicants that are taking the test for recertification, so it's crucial that they are given new tests as well to keep their memory fresh and experience relevant.

It's important to ensure that you use the study guide independently, as well as with this test. This is only half of the amount of questions that are going to be on the actual test, so there might be topics that weren't covered in every single question. If you refer to the study guide, you can see that there is a long list in each chapter of what you need to know before going in for the test. The practice exam will certainly help kick start your memory and give an idea of what to expect on the test day, but it's not going to provide you with every bit of information needed to pass the test.

When both are studied, as well as other important information, the test-taker has a much better chance of passing and receiving their certification. The more you study beforehand, the better prepared you will be on test day. Besides just learning the information, be sure that you are also ready by getting sleep, eating a healthy meal that will make you feel good before the test, and bring sharpened pencils. For most testing centers, a calculator will be provided as well, should you need one. Sometimes, you might be visually, or audio recorded, so don't let this distract you while taking the test.

At the end of the day, it is up to how focused and prepared an individual is for the test. The better this information is understood, the better the test-taker will be able to apply this knowledge to the test. Knowing different dates, names, and locations might seem tedious, but they can be key identifiers to remembering the bigger policies that they represent. Flashcards are a great way to study keywords, Acts, and laws. Studying with other people always helps as well. Although it can seem intimidating to enter the room on test day, what's waiting on the other side is incredibly rewarding.

This process is tough and can be draining for some. At the end of the day, there is an important goal to be achieved by different HRMs that are seeking their certification. It isn't about how much money is to be made or the responsibility and power that might come with the role. This information is important for passing the test, but it's also crucial for making sure that employees are being protected within their different work environments. It is up the HRM to make sure that this is happening.

Good luck!

PHR/SPHR Study Guide

Best PHR Test Prep to Help You Prepare for the PHR Exam! Get PHR Certification!

184

Introduction

Becoming a human resource manager can be a very fulfilling job, but there are certain requirements by different companies for the certification that are needed. The PHR Certification Exam is required in order to get an SPHR or PHR certificate. Not every human resource position requires this certification, though it can certainly help with different areas of expertise as well as making one applicant more experienced versus others.

The test is 225 multiple-choice questions, and they have to be answered within four hours. The questions are randomly generated, and each test is unique. In order to pass the test, a score of 500 out of 700 is required. The best way to ensure that the test is passed on exam day is to make sure you study, and you practice with other similar tests. There is no luck or chance involved, and the only way to be sure the information is known and understood is to apply it to concepts seen in various practice tests.

This book is best paired with the practice test associated, but the independent questions are important as well. In addition to passing the exam to receive certification, one must also have one of the following:

- 4 years professional HR position + a high school diploma

- 2 years professional HR position + bachelor's degree

- 1-year professional HR position + Master's degree or higher.

This study guide will help give an idea of the information that will be on the test, though it is not quite as long. In the other book that goes along with this one, in addition to practice questions, there will also be answers provided with an explanation in order to get a good understanding of what makes the answers correct.

The way this study guide is laid out is in the eight different sections of human resource management that the test will cover. Some parts are longer than others, but they each contain valuable information in order to pass the test.

The study guide will give bits of information as a way of reiteration, but it does not provide all information that might appear on the test.

Instead, it aims to provide a cohesive layout of what to expect, giving users a great guide for when it comes time to collate tools and materials needed in order to pass the test.

The first part of each chapter will go over the various information that will be needed in order to pass the exam. The first part of the chapter can act as a checklist for all of the information known. If you go through each of the things that are listed and ensure that those areas of study have been carefully looked over, you can be sure that you will pass the exam with flying colors.

The second half of each chapter will go over more specific information that is taken directly from previous test questions. Though there isn't likely going to be an exam that is exactly the same as one that has been given before, knowing which parts of certain areas of expertise that are included on the exam can help ensure that the tester is well prepared before going in for the process. The information will be very similar to what is in the practice guide, so it's important that this is all understood as best as possible.

The information is not to be memorized, but rather, learned and comprehended. Memorization will not help pass the test. The better someone can understand the actual concepts and laws of human resource management, the better they will be able to make sure they get high marks, as well as succeed in their position. Passing the exam is important but earning a certification and actually using it to help a company are much more important than what a score will read.

Still, it's crucial that the test is passed in the first place and following through with this study guide will help testers understand what they need to know before going in for the exam. Some parts might come naturally to certain testers while other sections require more attention. Everyone is different, so make sure to focus on what you need to know in order to get a good score. What might seem challenging to others could be simple information for you, but that doesn't mean that it should be ignored.

After going through this study guide, take the practice test if you have not already. If you have, it's encouraged that you go through it again to revise of important information that might present itself to you once again on test day.

When it comes time to show up for the test, make sure that you are well rested. Some people feel like they should stay up late to keep studying - worrying or having trouble sleeping over what score they might get. Prepare as much as you can for the test but cut yourself off the night before. there's a good chance that you'll do more harm than good if you try to stuff your brain with extra information. You might find yourself stressing over the mere fact that you cannot remember certain things. Don't cause yourself unnecessary panic. Instead, have a relaxing night focused on clearing your head and getting a good night's sleep so that you can show up fresh and alert for the test the next day.

Be prepared with your own pencil as well as a spare in case the first one breaks. You shouldn't need a calculator, but double check with your testing center just to be sure that they'll be providing one for you. Sometimes, you might be recorded, or at the very least, monitored while you take the test. Don't let this act as a distraction and instead focus on reading the questions thoroughly and picking the correct responses. The biggest reason why someone might fail the test is that they weren't prepared, or they got too hung up on specifics, not letting their knowledge do the work. Just remember that you can do this!

Good luck!

Chapter 1 – Business Management and Strategy

The business management and strategy section of this book are very important. It will lay out all aspects of a tester's ability to analyze internal, external, and business metric sources. There might be strategic questions that test a human resource manager's ability to apply correct knowledge to real-life situations. All areas of strategy and strategic management should be known in order to ensure high marks in this area of the test. Whether it's how a human resource manager spends their day, or what plan they're going to use to increase productivity, there is a lot to be known about the business management of a resource manager.

In order to be prepared, a tester must be able to apply industry best practices to general business environments. There will be questions on the test related to this kind of information, and not only will the tester have to know practical and fundamental meanings behind some of these practices, but they will also have to apply them to exemplary scenarios.

The tester should be prepared to understand what might make up a business's core values, mission statements, or overall goals. They should be able to analyze ethical and behavior expectations. This analyzation might come through on a personal level by looking at how different employees interact with each other. It might also be done with data analytics, in which the human resource manager can look at statistical information about their employees and determine a strategy for any conflict they are able to identify.

When it comes to business management and strategy, it is important to understand the importance that stakeholders have in a company. They also need to know the relationships that could be established in order to influence certain aspects of decision making that a manager might have to partake in. Knowing terms like cross-functional stakeholders and behavioral expectations will be important before going into this test.

A human resource manager also has to look at different data and determine what is useful and what is irrelevant. By doing this, they can better assess what the right conflict resolution to a problem will be. There are some things that can't be understood with data, but a well-trained human resource manager should know how to take all the information that was available to them and apply them to different real-life scenarios. Terms like attrition rates, time to fill, and ROI will all be important to not only memorize but to understand how they might apply in different examples.

Before going into the test, it is important to understand how different cultural impacts might affect business operations. Culture might be based on a certain race, lifestyle, or geographical location. All of these factors need to be considered when evaluating an employee for a specific job analysis. What steps would be taken to do this properly, and what are some of the laws that protect these employees? Information like this will be asked in a fundamental or functional sense, and it should also be understood in an applicable one as well.

How employees communicate with each other and with management is also incredibly important. Are they doing so in a professional manner or are they going about things in a way that could damage the integrity of the company? A skilled human resource manager will look at communication objectively and analyze whether it is productive or destructive.

One of the most important areas of knowledge a human resource manager should have are those ideas based around ethical and professional standards. At the core of what a human resource manager is responsible for is the maintenance of high standards of professionalism and ethics in order to make sure the needs of employees are being met while business strategies are still being properly implemented in a way that will help the company grow and not keep it straggling behind.

What differs from the test now versus ten or so years ago is the use of technology in order to report or record different aspects of human resource management. Before going into the test, familiarize yourself with the quantitative data collecting methods that are popular now among human resource management. Specific brands might not be mentioned, but overall, the tools that someone might use, such as HRIS, are important to understanding to make sure that all questions can be properly answered.

The next section will cover more specific information that has been taken directly from old tests. This information might not be an exact replica of what is to be expected on the new and current exam, however, it will give readers a good idea of the kind of information that the test creators had in mind when writing up questions. This information is the basis for what you should be studying, among other things, in relation to this chapter's title.

Polygraph Tests

In terms of the strategic role of a Human Resources manager, issuing polygraph tests to all employees would not be included. A human resources manager would, however, plan, discover organizational objectives, and determine an employee's resistance to a geographical location.

There are many strategic roles that an HR manager has, but polygraph testing is not one of them. This can be remembered by looking at the core administrative functions of a human resource manager. These include training and development, benefits administration, recruitment, compensation analysis, and general employee administration. Though a polygraph test might occur in one of these stages, it would not be the responsibility of a human resource manager.

Recruitment involves putting the word out there of the job, and initial interviews and background checks. After that, compensation is decided for an individual employee. The benefits are considered at this stage as well.

Once that has all been settled, the HRM will guide an employee through their training and development, and later maintain general employee administration. None of these steps would include giving an employee a polygraph test.

Polygraph tests are rarely done as it is, even in the recruitment phase. If they are given, then a professional will be there to oversee the test is given properly. As a human resource manager, you won't be expected to give a polygraph test.

Forecasting

Forecasting HR demands can be done with productivity ratios, statistical regression analysis, or simulation models. Any of these mathematical methods would aid in forecasting, and an HR manager is also not limited to these three methods. Forecasting is becoming more relevant as more tools emerge for different resource managers. There are always new innovations to collect and analyze data, so it is important to stay informed on the tools out there that could help grow and develop a business.

As HR managers look to the future, they will have to expect that they might have to deal with an older workforce. This is especially true for positions that are long term. As time goes on, the workforce will always become more diverse.

The amount of the workforce that is entry-level or one that lacks skills doesn't have as much of a differentiation through an HR manager's position. Forecasting involves figuring out labor supply projections, staffing requirement projections, and an understanding of external conditions. Forecasting does not include an analysis of a job. The world is changing every single day, but that doesn't mean that everything is always rapidly different.

There are certain HRM trends that are going to stay the same, and that includes workers that lack skills as well as some entry-level workers. Innovations in education, as well as training programs, will alter the way HR managers hire and who they will hire, but what will differ most in the short-term goals of a human resource manager is how they will handle their employees that are older than the original workforce that has been dealt with.

At its core, forecasting is when labor needs are projected and predicted, and the effects that might have on a business are analyzed as well. Once this basic idea has been discovered, it is then up to the HRM to hire staff in order to properly ensure that the labor needs are being met.

The HRM does more than just hire, they also have to ensure that they are taking care of the needs of their current employees while simultaneously looking at how new hirings will affect the current status of work. The HRM also needs to check up on how this labor cost is going to affect other parts of the business, such as sales, office space, and the money needed for different benefits, compensations, and insurances. Forecasting is like looking at the weather forecast, but for HRM, the storm is new hires.

There are many different methods that a human resource manager can use to forecast their individual business. For the most part, it would start with setting a goal of what needs to be predicted. Is the HRM looking at an estimation of market demand, or trying to resolve employee turnover? A productivity ratio would assess the number of employees it takes to get a certain task done.

This would be helpful in determining how many employees are needed to be hired, or what employees could be moved from certain departments. Each of these mathematical methods has a purpose when it comes to forecasting, and it is up to the HRM to make sure that they are looking out for what the best model for prediction would be. The more aware a human resource manager is of all the mathematical methods there are to aid in forecasting, the better they will be able to make predictions for their company.

Strategic Management

Skill variety, task significance, and autonomy are all included in a job characteristics model. Not all are required, but they all qualify as answers to the question. A job characteristics model is comprised of five core job characteristics. These include skill variety, task significance, task identity, autonomy, and feedback. From these five characteristics, there are five work-related outcomes that could be a result of this model as well.;

This includes [A] motivation, [B] performance, [C] absenteeism, [D] satisfaction, and [E] turnover. The job characteristics model is a representation of the job characteristics theory. This model has been modified, though the core values are what remains important to HR managers.

An Ishikawa diagram can also be described as a cause and effect diagram. An Ishikawa diagram is one that was created by Kaoru Ishikawa. All of the types of Ishikawa diagrams show the causes that a specific event might have. A herringbone, Fishikawa, fishbone diagram, or cause-and-effect diagram are all interchangeable terms and are known as Ishikawa diagrams.

Ishikawa forces those that create the diagram to really look at all the causes of a certain problem. By doing this, a human resource manager might find a problem causer that they didn't expect, perhaps in a small department they weren't giving attention to. By looking at more obvious causes and effects, you might miss out on the small things that are really causing serious damage in a certain industry.

Relocation

If someone in a managerial position is analyzing geographic and competitive concerns, they must consider a particular employee's willingness to relocate to certain geographical locations. Restructuring organizationally might be considered after the employee's desires to relocate are learned.

Foot traffic and work-family balance don't affect what an HR manager might decide. Not every company has the opportunity for relocation, but when it is presented, the HRM needs to ensure there is a proper program that will help this situation. A relocation scenario would involve a relocation package that would present the benefits to an employee that was eligible for relocation.

The better prepared you are as a human resource manager for relocation services, the smoother everything will go over in this sometimes-challenging position. A human resource manager has to be aware of all the possibilities, benefits, and risks that are involved in a potential relocation. Relocation is not meant to be confused with travel opportunities for employees as well.

Organizations

Organization development can be divided into three different categories – technological, interpersonal, and structural. The process to analyze and identify how much human resources is needed is known as human resource planning. This helps make sure an organization can meet its goal while determining how many human resources is needed to meet the objectives.

A human resource manager is responsible for looking over all other staff and making sure their needs are taken care of, they're being compensated, and all rules are being followed in order to make sure that things continue to run smoothly.

A human resource manager is also responsible for themselves! They have to make sure that they are identifying the need for human resources, what the future might require, and how different costs could be cut in their own department. Human resource planning is important in connecting the overall organization to the actual human resources.

Organization development refers to what it

sounds like – how to develop organizational practices within a business. It starts with a technological aspect. What can be computerized, digitized, and added online to a storage system? How can technology overall improve organization and the work efforts of the different employees?

The next stage is interpersonal. What is going on with the employees of a company that can be changed to be better organized? Finally, a structural standpoint should be discovered for human resource managers that want to achieve better organization development. What overall, in the structure of the company, needs to be developed in order for optimal organization to be achieved?

Life Cycle

Of the stages of a life cycle of human resource development, middle age is not a stage. Growth, maturity, and introduction are all considered stages. Most businesses go through four stages that affect how they will operate. The first is growth. Whether this is done overnight or over a decade, all businesses go through a period of growth.

In this stage, a human resource manager would be responsible for overseeing the hiring, recruitment, and evaluation of different employees. As a company goes through the second stage, maturity, the HRM will help in maintaining employee needs, ensuring that different aspects of compensation are being taken care of. This might also include the promotion of a business. The third stage, one that not all businesses will meet, is rebirth.

This is when the company gets a new face, whether it's from rebranding, relocating, or recruiting new managerial staff. The HRM in this process will be responsible for looking back on the company and evaluating what needs to be done to make sure it runs more efficiently. The final stage is decline, and in this stage, if it happens, the HRM would be responsible for cutting employees and other costs that would help keep the business alive as long as possible. Downsizing is when there is a reduction in the size of an overall workforce organization.

Downsizing can occur for many different reasons. It might be to cut the costs of a struggling company. There might be a way to increase profit instead, looking at positions that don't hold as much value as others.

Downsizing can also happen during moments of rebranding when computers or other services are used in place of different things that previous employees did. Downsizing staff can be risky for those that have to lose their jobs, but also for the employees left.

They might fear that they are next in line to get cut, or they might have trouble taking on new responsibilities that the other employees left behind. It is not the final decision of a human resource manager to downsize, but it is up to them to make sure that this operation goes smoothly, and no one suffers more than they have to.

Strategy

HRIS stands for Human Resource Information System. This might also be known as a human resource management system (HUMAN RESOURCE MANAGERS). This is in reference to the software and technology used by human resource managers. There is not one specific program necessary for all human resource managers to use, though there are certain favorites.

It's important to know the acronym in order to determine if a technological or interpersonal issue is being discussed in terms of strategic human resource management. Having electronic HR management documentations allows for certain managers to better look over past and future proceedings to ensure that no steps are being missed, and all information is presented.

As more human resource innovation emerges, so does the need to stay technologically advanced. The more aware one human resource department can be with their technologic knowledge, the better equipped they will be to analyze and process relevant data to ensure they are going about things in efficient ways.

Sometimes, this might include collecting data on employee productivity and using numbers in comparable situations. This might not have been seen as much in previous tests, and it can only be assumed that technological innovation as a resource to analyze positions will become more relevant in the following years.

Succession Plans can be described as an anticipation of the staffing requirements a managerial position holds with the development of high-quality employees in order to meet these needs stated. HR Succession Planning looks at employees that can fill the positions of those in a managerial position when they can no longer fulfill their duties.

This might mean setting others up to take over when someone quits or retires. By properly succession planning, human resource managers can make transitions smooth when those who might have held a certain position for decades finally leave. New management can be very tricky for many businesses to recover from, but it is something that can be done without much destruction if there is a proper succession plan in place.

The dislikes of an employee are not part of the development of a business strategy. When developing a business strategy, it is important to look at both the external factors that might threaten a business, as well as the internal systems that could provide strengths and weaknesses to a company.

An external scan might include things like environmental factors, demographics, competitors, and basic geographical locations. Internal scanning requires businesses to look inward, seeing what weaknesses might hold them back. This could be things such as not having enough of a budget, lack of experience, or unavailability of certain resources. These two scans are very important in order to produce a quality business strategy.

Hofstede's IBM Employee Study

The five dimensions taken from Hofstede's IBM employee study are: ①uncertainty avoidance, ②long-term orientation, ③power distance, ④individualism, ⑤masculine/feminine.

In Hofstede's cultural dimensions, an uncertainty avoidance is in reference to how a society is able to tolerate all of the uncertainty that comes along with day to day operations. You can never predict if there's going to be a hurricane that wipes out a plant, or a manager that needs to take sick leave for a month at a time.

We might be able to make certain predictions based on guesses, but there will always be a level of uncertainty. Uncertainty avoidance is in reference to how the members of a culture program might feel about their comfortability level in various situations that don't seem to have any structure.

Hofstede's IBM employee study aimed to see how different cultures were affected by systematic differences. His analysis produced four dimensions on which national cultures differentiated. The first was ① uncertainty avoidance. This is how comfortable certain people are with change or the uncertainty level of different aspects of life. ② The second is long-term orientation, or how someone might plan for the future.

The ③ third is power distance, which is how others influence those around them, and what level they're comfortable doing so. How willing are people to accept inequality? The fourth is ④ individualism, which is all about personal needs and whether or not someone's personal goals are being met versus the overall goals of the organization. The final dimension is ⑤ masculine/feminine, which looks at how masculine and feminine rules determine different cultural aspects.

Types of Organizations

An organization that would be considered a "prospector" would include the HR practice of external staffing. External staffing is when there is a recruitment of those outside a

210

company to fill positions needed, rather than looking within a company.

This is different than just hiring for an open position. Sometimes, it means looking elsewhere for a manager rather than at a staff that might have years of experience. A company that is a prospective one is one that is looking for innovations and new ways to boost their product or service. They might consider external staffing as a way to bring fresh life into a company that desperately needs a change.

Identifying the type of organization that makes up a company is important for human resource managers so they can properly assess and analyze all the tools needed to help make sure that the company is continually growing and positively expanding.

Chapter 2 – Workforce Planning and Employment

Workforce planning and employment refer to the way that a human resource manager goes about planning their strategies that are going to be used to reach their goals and finding the right employees to help do this. This section covers any recruitment, promotion, hiring, organizing, and orientation, as well as an exit strategy that might be integrated into a business for when an employee decides to go their separate ways.

A human resource manager knows that success comes from the team that helps drive a business and not always just who is on top. A human resource manager will do a fair job in the hiring process, abiding by all the rules put in place to protect the people from any unfair discrimination when it comes time to find the right position.

This section will also look at how much human resources a business might need. Not only do human resource managers have to plan for the company, but they also have to look out for themselves and their own schedules.

A human resource manager will know what to look for when it comes time to fill staff. The right people will have the right set of skills, and anything they lack can be made up for in the training process that a human resource manager might help to create.

This section on the test will go over the responsibilities that a human resource manager might have. Though responsibilities might change slightly from one position to the next, there are some key aspects of the human resource position that will hold true no matter where someone might be working. They are responsible for workforce planning and the employee activities that occur, as well as making sure all of this is legal and compliant with any federal laws in place.

This section of the test might force the tester to use their knowledge of these federal laws and apply them to real-life scenarios. Some laws can be up for interpretation, and in a real-world scenario, there might be leniency one way or another. What's most important is looking at the core values and ideas that make up a law, ensuring that the basic understanding is known so application can be done on the test.

Employment law is a part that can trip up a lot of people on the test, so if this is an area of struggle, it's important to put emphasis on this during the study. There are many different sections of laws that change and amend throughout time, so staying up to date with all of these is crucial for anyone that wants to pass the test.

Uniform guidelines, employment law, the civil rights act, and other standards that are legally mandated are all things that should be known. Even for those that don't ever expect to work in a large company, or someone that has a job in a location that doesn't require uniforms, it's important to be aware of all these different types of rules and regulations in order to have a decent understanding when it comes time to take the test.

Different types of validity should be known, such as predictive validity, construct validity, content validity, and criterion-related validity. These forms might get mixed up on the test, so it's crucial to not get caught up too much with various small differences in words.

Governing EEO laws might make up a large section of the test. It's different every year but focusing on this particular section has been consistent among many different test taker's tales. Title VII is a big one to study, but we will also touch on it a little more in depth in this book.

Quid Pro Quo

A quid pro quo can also mean "this for that." Sympathy, whistleblowing, and reasonable person are all terms that have different meanings. A quid pro quo is a favor that is given but with the expectation that the same favor will be returned or repaid in another way. "This for that," is another way to explain this, as you might say, "if you give me this, I'll give you that."

In terms of human resource management, this is something that has to be familiar in order to ensure it is not taking place in the workplace. Most often, a quid pro quo is seen when a manager offers something to an employee in return for a sexual, or otherwise illegal, favor. This form of harassment can be very dangerous, as the employee might feel fearful to tell the HRM of the harassment out of fear of losing their job. Unfortunately, a quid pro quo is the most common form of harassment in different work environments.

There are many other forms of harassment, threat, and blackmailing that might be done in a work environment. Those taking this test should be sure that they are aware of all the steps involved in a harassment case. It starts with identifying the problem and figuring out if it qualifies as a reportable case. After that there needs to be a mediation between those that were involved, with a conflict resolution to follow. There might be different policies in place depending on different organizations, but those taking this exam should still make sure they have a general understanding of harassment and what's needed to properly handle this situation.

FLSA

According to the United States Department of Labor's website, "The Fair Labor Standards Act (FLSA) establishes minimum wage, overtime pay, recordkeeping, and child labor standards affecting full-time and part-time workers in the private sector and in Federal, State, and local governments."

This is just one of the many parts of the Act, and though not all sections need to be memorized, they do need to be known. It is better to memorize them in order to catch sneaky questions that might switch around wording, but really, a basic understanding of when the law or amendment came about, what inspired its creation, and how it currently affects workers should help the exam taker to properly answer any question pertaining to a legal issue.

This would protect any overtime pay that an employee deserves and the record keeping involved in their employment history. It would also include administrative concerns, as well as an employee's status, in reference to if they are part-time, temporary, or on a working visa. The FLSA does not include any retirement plans, as that would be more between the relationship with the employee and their employer, or with a different independent retirement plan they are working with.

Most employees are protected by the FLSA, meaning they are nonexempt. Nonexempt positions are entitled to overtime pay. If more than 40 hours of work are given in a pay week, that employee is entitled to pay that is at least time and a half, though some companies might have different overtime incentives.

Either way, the FLSA mandates that nonexempt employees receive what they deserve when overtime work is given. Exempt employees are those that earn a salary of $23,660 per year, or more. These workers are not protected under the FLSA, though many companies will still offer overtime pay if a certain number of hours are worked, as an employee incentive.

If someone partially works their weekly hours as well as a combination of cashing in on vacation hours for their weekly salary, they wouldn't be entitled to overtime, even if they got paid for more than forty hours in a week.

For example, someone that works 39 hours in a week and uses 2 vacation hours would not be entitled to that extra hour of overtime pay, since the hours weren't technically worked. Getting paid time and a half doesn't qualify as overtime either.

Overtime is only given when someone actually works more than forty hours in a week, and they are nonexempt. There might be situational examples on the test that could slip up some takers, so it's important to be aware of how to apply these rules and laws to real-life situations.

Many employees are given a salary, which is usually an amount slightly higher than what the average total amount of a 40-hour minimum wage paycheck would be. A salary is usually referred to in annual terms, meaning if a person gets paid $1,000 a week, they have a salary of $52,000 a year.

This form of payment is mostly given to professional and white-collar workers. Not everyone in a company gets paid the same, so some employees might make a salary while others receive an hourly fee. Getting paid a salary will usually be part of a compensation package that also includes other benefits, such as paid vacation, healthcare, and other forms of insurance.

The FLSA regulates overtime pay, recordkeeping, administrative concerns, and employee status. FLSA is not responsible for the retirement plans of employees, work-related injuries that might have caused an employee to take out worker's compensation, or the familial affairs of their employees.

The Fair Labor Standards Act is one of the most important acts for Human resource managers to be aware of in order to ensure their employees most basic rights are being met within a corporation. This includes adhering to a federal minimum wage that must be met, with very few exceptions in place.

This also makes sure recordkeeping is being kept and properly recorded in order to ensure that the rights of employees are being protected. The FLSA is also responsible for establishing child labor standards and restricted hours for children of a certain age. Though there are more important factors within this act, these are the most basic to understand and remember.

Nonexempt positions, according to the Fair Labor Standards Act, would be positions that perform clerical, routine, or manual work during a percentage of their time. Overtime pay, children's work hours, and minimum wage regulation are all protected under The Fair Labor Standards Act.

Short-term disability would be how a pregnancy is treated according to The Pregnancy Discrimination Act of 1978. The Pregnancy Discrimination Act of 1978 states:

> "The terms 'because of sex' or 'on the basis of sex' include, but are not limited to, because of or on the basis of pregnancy, childbirth, or related medical conditions; and women affected by pregnancy, childbirth, or related

medical conditions shall be treated the same for all employment-related purposes, including receipt of benefits under fringe benefit programs, as other persons not so affected but similar in their ability or inability to work."

This protects employees that are pregnant or choose to become pregnant from discrimination. In order to go through the proper paperwork, Human resource managers are encouraged to treat a pregnancy such as a short-term disability, meaning that the employee will be back to work after a period of time has been taken off. This will be seen in many sections throughout this quiz.

Learning about the compensation, bonuses, and benefits that new parents and families in general receive is important in order to pass the test. This is a huge part of human resource management, so it is going to appear on the test often as well.

Job Analysis

A job analysis does not include obligations

certain tasks carry. A job analysis would include investigating a way to gather information about the content of a job, a systematic method of analyzing human requirements, and the context in which jobs are performed.

In a job analysis, the certain duties required by a position are identified. Looking at what duties, jobs, specifications, and responsibilities of a position are important in order to collect data and analyze what parts of a position are required, and which can be cut down. Is a person getting paid enough, or is there a way that hours should be cut in order to save money?

By figuring out an in-depth job analysis, human resource managers are able to decide who is the best fit for a certain position and who would be better suited elsewhere. A job analysis differs from a job description in that it is more in-depth, and a process performed by a human resource manager, rather than a job description that would simply list the duties and expectations of a certain position.

During a job analysis, a human resource manager might need to determine what the most important position in a company might be. In order to do this, they might use a point factor method. This would first involve selecting a job cluster of the company. From there, the HRM would pick out factors of each of those jobs and determine a degree or scale of what makes these compensable.

Different weights would be given to different aspects, and from there, a score can be added to determine which positions hold the most value. This is always important to do to ensure that fair labor is being given as well as fair compensation. Doing this once doesn't mean that it doesn't need to be done again. It should be something included annually, if not more.

Job Description

A job description is necessary in order to weed out potential candidates that wouldn't be a good fit for a position. At any given time, there are many people on the hunt for a new job. Not every single one of these people is going to be a good fit, or even qualified, for certain positions.

The more detailed a job description, the better a chance for employees that are actually good candidates to get an interview time in. A job description will list the responsibilities of that position, and their purpose and relation to other positions in the company. How often someone is interacting with the public or working in a team will usually be specified in a job description as well.

The qualifications needed, whether it's a degree, certificate, or a number of years of experience will also help make a job description more detailed to ensure that only those that qualify will be able to get an interview slot. A job description might include a salary listed, though this is often something that is going to be discussed after the first interview when abilities are determined.

Predictive Validity

Predictive validity best describes an index number that is given to the relationship between a predictor and the criterion variable. As a human resource manager, it is important to understand all the ways that different employee data analytics can be predicted and analyzed. All different forms of validity should be studied and understood so they could be properly applied in different situational examples.

Depending on a human resource manager's

objective, there is likely going to be a different method of achieving the information that is desired. Sometimes, this information isn't going to be completely accurate, but in other instances, it might even be spot on. Predictive validity refers to the efficiency in which a test is conducted and the information that is measured. Predictive validity looks at how that tool was used to achieve the desired information, and whether or not it did the job it needed to do. By doing this assessment, it can be better determined how results might be achieved better the next time a human resource manager is collecting data. Looking towards the future of a company is an important role for a human resource manager, and predictive validity can help assess the productivity of an HRM's fortune-telling abilities.

Discrimination

Sex, racial and ethnic, and age discrimination are all considered types of employment discrimination. Hiring only young, thin, attractive women can be a form of disparate treatment. Sexual harassment and intentional treatment might also be exhibited in addition to this, but they aren't necessarily inherent or the same thing as disparate treatment. Disparate treatment and disparate impact are two different terms that need to be differentiated, as there might be a trick question that combines the two on the actual exam.

Disparate treatment is when there is an intentional discrimination in the employment process. It might involve testing certain sexes or minorities in different areas rather than testing all employees equally. Someone that wants to only give background checks to African American applicants would be practicing disparate treatment.

Disparate impact occurs when there is more of an unintentional discriminatory practice in place. A disparate impact is one that might eliminate a certain protected group during the interview process because of a requirement that would likely make them ineligible. For example, imagine an electrician who's reaching the age of retirement, but he's not ready to end his career.

The electrician's managers fire him and justify doing so because he received several complaints. They are allowed to fire him, however, if there are several other employees that are younger than him with the same amount of complaints, and the company doesn't fire them, they are exhibiting a disparate impact.

Discrimination doesn't stop at the hiring process. Discrimination comes in many different forms, is sometimes obvious and other times challenging to identify. An experienced HRM will know how to spot discrimination and what makes up a discriminatory act. If any discrimination is even sensed, it is always worth investigating.

Those that are discriminated against belong to a protected class, which includes, women, minorities, and those part of the LGBTQA community. Discrimination could be as subtle as not giving off a requested vacation day to someone in a protected group, or it could be as large as firing someone because they are homosexual.

No matter the degree of discrimination that an employee faces, action must be taken by a human resource manager to protect the worker's rights and the integrity of the company.

Interview

A targeted selection interview uses questions to investigate what an employer might have done in other positions that are related to the job being interviewed for. A group, phone, and situational interview all use different methods of gaining information about potential candidates.

A target selection interview allows the employer to determine the specific points of a job and how well a person might be able to fulfill those duties. In a target selection interview, the previous jobs and duties that someone went through in their past positions will provide examples of how they might perform in the next position.

Not only does this allow an employer to better determine if the person they are interviewing is right for the position, but the potential candidate also has the opportunity to meet management and see if the job is really something that they are interested in after all.

These are common types of interviews, though there are many others that have their own benefits as well. It's important to go into the test knowing about all the different types of interviews in order to ensure that preparation is met for the test.

A behavioral interview is one that takes place in the hiring process when an employee gets asked about their past behavior. A behavioral interview is probably one of the most common types of interviews that many employers use to get to know different candidates.

In a behavioral job interview, candidates will be asked about how they might have reacted in previous situations that aren't even related to the workforce. This is to gauge what they might be like in different situations.

If someone is making a judgment, for instance, in a job interview a rating might be done, and that judge lets their personal interest affect their professional score, this would be known as a rater's bias.

As a human resource manager, it is crucial that personal ideas don't interfere with a rating that might be given to an employee on a professional level. For instance, if an employee has a certain tattoo of a band that the HRM doesn't like, this should not affect the way they perceive that employee.

If tattoos are permitted, nothing about the personal taste of that employee should affect how a human resource manager treats them, so, during an employee review, small personal distaste among the two should be kept out of the equation. If not, a rater's bias might occur, giving the employee an unfair disadvantage.

Performance Appraisal

Performance appraisal is another way of saying "employee evaluation." Job design, HR strategic management, and 360-degree feedback all refer to different things but don't mean the same thing as an employee evaluation.

Performance appraisal is used to measure an employee's adherence to the performance standards put in place. A performance appraisal gives an employer the chance to address the issue of an employee failing to adhere to the performance standards.

This appraisal might happen yearly, monthly, or not at all, depending on the company. An appraisal has no legal definitions, and what might be involved is different among various institutions. It might be done with a direct supervisor, or it could occur with an entire group of the heads of the department.

It's important for a human resource manager to be aware of the various things that might be discussed within a performance appraisal, so they can ensure they're being fairly and properly conducted.

In a performance appraisal, an employee's contribution to the company, as well as overall job performance, will be evaluated. Because this is similar to an employee evaluation, the two terms can be interchangeable.

Sometimes, these reviews might happen annually, or they could happen every month. Sometimes, reviews will be face to face, but they also might be completed through documents. The point of doing a performance evaluation is to ensure there aren't any problems that need addressing between management and an employee.

Areas of strength and weakness can be discussed in a performance review, allowing for both the company and the employee to continually grow. There are three key functions that must be addressed in a performance appraisal. The first one being feedback and needs to be provided to both the employee and the employer.

What does each think of the others'
performance? The second key function is to
allow for the modification of working habits or
a work environment. The third function is one
that provides data to the manager and the
HRM to use for future assessment. It gives a
basis for comparison so that each job
assessment becomes more functional.

Types of Employment

Job sharing is an example of an alternative
work schedule. Self-employment, self-directed
task force, and remote are all terms that have
different meanings than "alternative work
schedule."

An alternative work schedule is one that
includes a full work week completed in a
condensed amount of time. Instead of working
a full 40-hour workweek within five days, it
might be completed in three. Any form of a
compressed work schedule would be
considered alternative.

Job sharing is in reference to more than one
employee that shares the duties of a full-time

position. For example, two people might work 20-hours within a three-day period, completing the tasks that someone might have needed 5 days for if it were one full-time employee.

Working remotely could be considered an alternative work schedule, but only if that employee chooses to do their full-time work within a short period of time.

An independent contractor is someone that is contracted by an employer for a certain duty, task, operation, or goal. They are hired on as a non-employee and are only brought in to take on that certain task. Sometimes, an independent contractor might work for a company more than once if the employer enjoys their work.

For example, someone working at a video production company might get hired to help light sets, but they wouldn't be given a consistent position and would instead continue to find their own work elsewhere. They would likely bring some of their own lights and would have to make sure all their projects would allow for a new position to be taken on. They might never hear from the employer again for another project, or they might get hired every other month when their work is needed.

A closed shop refers to a union that requires hired employees to join the union upon hiring. It does not refer to an old union, a closed store, or a union that does not allow any new members.

In a closed shop, there will be a predetermined agreement between the union and employers in which they will only hire those that are going to become union members. In a closed shop, employees must also remain a member of that union, meaning from beginning to end, they are in agreement with their union.

By doing this, it keeps the union stronger and allows for the union to also have more of a say in who is a good candidate to hire. This is not always the case with how unions work, so it is important to know all of the different kinds of unions and what agreements come along with each different type of union shops.

Chapter 3 – Total Rewards

Total rewards refer to any and all ways that an employee receives what they need in order to compensate them correctly for the work that they have done. The reason we all work is just to get paid, so this area is certainly important for human resource managers to be aware of all areas of compensation, benefits, and payroll. Sometimes, a human resource manager might be directly responsible for payroll, or there might be a team of people implemented to send out paychecks. Either way, it's crucial that a human resource manager is aware and understanding of all aspects of payroll.

Aside from just how someone makes their money, a human resource manager needs to know what different amounts of compensation employees are entitled to when they experience different levels of injury, promotions, or other events that entitle them to a different amount of pay than what they are used to.

Human resource managers should also be aware of how to maintain fair pay and how to look into a case in which someone is not receiving what they are owed. They will have to oversee the different ways in which someone might be compensated while making sure that everything is handled professionally and legally.

Sometimes, a human resource manager might be a part of different negotiations that involve getting paid more or receiving more benefits. They must know the procedures that are put in place in order to protect workers as well as the employers that are doing the check-signing.

All aspects of compensation programs, rather it's implementation, promotion, management, or compliance, is dealt with in a human resource department. Giving compensation is important because it is what the employee usually cares about the most. All federal laws need to be followed during this process as well, so the test taker needs to be aware of different rules and regulations that affect employee's compensation amounts.

It is also up to the human resource manager to promote other forms of cash rewards. There might be a way to pay off tuition within a working environment, or volunteering time could count towards bonuses as well. There might be different kinds of workplace amenities which could include a gym or healthy snacks that would count towards the compensation that an employee receives. It is also the duty of the human resource manager to give out different rewards bonuses, such as extra store credit when a certain sales goal has been met.

A human resource manager needs to know all about the different implementation of an employee's benefit program. This means making oneself aware of the different healthcare plans available, and what sort of vision/dental/or retirement plans that a person is entitled to within their company.

Budgeting is going to be a large part of a human resource manager's job, as well as a subject that will be discussed on the test. The more a human resource manager knows about this subject, the better they will be able to run the company efficiently. Budgeting directly ties into payroll, and there are many laws that also protect payroll that a human resource manager needs to be aware of.

There are some specific accounting practices that a human resource manager might be in charge of as well, in association with different compensation packages. All forms of accounting need to be understood in order to ensure that those taking the test are able to pass this particular area.

Indirect and direct compensation need to be differentiated, and non-cash compensation should be understood at the core as well. Benchmarking compensation and benefits, and the methods in which these two are aligned should be understood as best as possible.

Some of these aspects will be discussed in the following sections, but anything that there isn't time to touch on should be closely studied for anything that a test taker is not aware of.

Compensation

Transportation costs would not be addressed in a compensation program. Legal compliance, equity for employees, and cost-effectiveness might all be factors that would be addressed in a compensation program.

A compensation program would include how and what an employee is going to be paid. It might include any legal compliances that the company would cover for their employees. There is also a chance that it would consider different equity for employees, as well as the cost-effectiveness of certain other programs that exist within the compensation plan.

A human resource manager would be responsible for overlooking different compensation programs and would have to be sure that they are creating something cost-efficient and fair enough to cover what the employee is entitled to.

Executives receive more variety of compensation programs that are available as compared to the other employees in the firm. Executives do not receive a strict flat rate among the top ten highest paid employees in a company, nor do they receive a paycheck exempt from federal taxes. An executive might get compensation paid quarterly, but this is not necessarily an executive standard.

Executives are paid much differently because there is usually an element of incentive involved for the executive to perform, or encourage their staff to perform, more efficiently to turn a higher profit. Long-term cash incentives are involved in executive corporations, as well as global compensation.

There is no standard for an executive compensation, but it will typically involve many more benefits and luxuries than other employees in the company. The pay packages are much more diverse, and it's important to know what might be involved in order to differentiate from other employee compensation programs.

Long-term incentive pay is best described as a form of direct compensation. Direct compensation refers to any instance that money is directly paid to an employee. Most often, this includes salaries, wages, commission, and bonuses. Indirect payment involves something that isn't liquid paid to an employee. This would include maternity leave, other flexible benefits, and worker's compensation. Long-term incentive pay refers to anytime an executive is paid for achieving certain goals or milestones. These usually include strategic objectives and performance goals that will motivate the executive to increase profit among the company, therefore promising long-term incentive pay. What makes up a long-term incentive pay program is different, but it is still referred to as a form of direct compensation.

Unemployment compensation covers when employees are laid off even though it's not their fault whatsoever. In some cases, a human resource manager might be involved in the process of laying off different employees. This is an unfortunate time, but there is at least compensation to be given to employees that experience this layoff. This is referred to as unemployment compensation.

This is usually calculated by taking gross wages in two different quarters, dividing by 2, and multiplying by .03. Unemployment does not pay as much as normal compensation, and the terms will be different based on an employee's length with a company, ability to find more work, and how much they had to be made within the rest of the year. Sometimes, severance packages are given during layoffs, but these are not to be interchanged with unemployment compensation.

Indirect Compensation

Indirect compensation is a way of stating benefits. The bonuses that come along with a company would be referred to as the indirect benefits that are associated with a certain position. Unpaid leave, social security benefits, and differential pay would all present themselves in cash or check form.

Indirect compensation might be the price taken off a medical bill that was covered by insurance, or a bonus like a company car or phone that the employee can use at their own discretion. Different forms of indirect compensation should be known in order to pass the test better.

The Equal Pay Act

The Equal Pay act will help with compensation associated with discrimination. According to the U.S. Equal Employment Opportunity Commission, the Equal Pay Act of 1963, "prohibits sex-based wage discrimination between men and women in the same establishment who perform jobs that require substantially equal skill, effort and responsibility under similar working conditions." This was enacted in 1963 in order to protect the rights of workers. Though dates can sometimes be hard to memorize, the test often asks for different dates as a way to test memorization skills of the test taker.

The Equal Pay act was put in place in order to make sure that everyone would be paid fairly in an organization no matter their race, sex, age, or any other reason that someone might discriminate against them. However, there are some exceptions that define that certain differences in pay aren't considered wage discrimination. One exception is seniority pay.

This means that certain people that were in a company longer than others are entitled to a higher pay because of their seniority. A merit system is another exemption from a different wage gap, meaning that an employee's job performance will determine how they might get paid. Certain factors within these exemptions might be subjective, which is where the importance of a human resource manager comes in to make sure that the exemption is legitimate.

The Equal Pay Act was put in place in order to make sure that those with the same skills, effort, and responsibilities are protected. An exemption from The Equal Pay act would be overtime.

An equal employment opportunity survey is one that might be required to be filled out by various institutions on a regular basis. For example, a bank that issues U.S. savings bonds might be required to fill one out annually. This survey will help determine the different demographics of a job, including what race, ethnicity, and gender are present in a certain work environment, ensuring there is equality among employees and the various positions.

By implementing this survey in different positions, employees can be sure that they will be protected from discrimination, and the public that might be involved with these positions also can be certain that there will be a diverse workforce that won't discriminate against them either.

Payroll

Payroll involves how a person might get paid. Sometimes, this might be done through different programs, or it might involve straight up handing someone a signed check. No matter what the method is for how an employee might get paid, it's crucial that the human resource manager understands every level of this.

That might include taking out a certain amount of taxes, or it could also be in reference to other exemptions that are removed from a paycheck. There are many different aspects that protect a worker's salary and wage, so the human resource manager needs to know all of these in order to properly assess whether or not someone is being paid correctly.

The Davis-Bacon Act of 1931

The Davis-Bacon Act of 1931 is most relevant to companies that are firms currently engaged with federal construction projects, and only those whose projects exceed the cost of $2,000. This also states that the "prevailing wage," is a rate that must be paid.

The Davis-Bacon Act is important in protecting federal workers, ensuring that they are entitled to minimum wage standards even when not working full-time positions. This Act emerged in 1931 and states, "contractors and subcontractors performing on federally funded or assisted contracts in excess of $2,000 for the construction, alteration, or repair (including painting and decorating) of public buildings or public works."

Person-Based Pay System

A system that doesn't pay employees based on the tasks that are currently performed, but rather based on what employees are capable of doing is known as a person-based pay system.

A person-based pay system might involve an employee getting paid more based on the experience or skill level that they have. This might also include getting paid more based on a certification or degree that someone has. It cannot be based on any sort of discriminatory reasons, such as a person's age or sex.

Benefits

Holiday bonuses would not be considered legally mandated benefits. Social security, worker's compensation, and unemployment compensation would all be considered legally mandated benefits.

Legally-mandated benefits, also known as legally required benefits, is anything that is required to cover the treatment of different aspects of healthcare. These might include social security, Medicare, or the Federal Insurance Contributions Act (FICA). This is what's often taken out of employee's checks in order to go to other services.

Holiday bonuses and other forms of compensation that are "extra" features would not be considered legally mandated benefits. This can be remembered by thinking of the basic needs that need to be taken care of. Lower-income families, the elderly, and those that are disabled still need to receive money, which is where legally mandated benefits would come into effect.

Packages

A benefits package can be great for the employee receiving this form of compensation. Having insurance brings peace of mind as well as many other factors that would improve a worker's mood while working. Aside from benefits to the employee, there is also a good reason that a company would want to offer their employees a fair benefits package. The main reason would be that it would help reduce turnover. Employees that are satisfied with the amount they are receiving and the protection that surrounds their health as well of their families will be more likely to stick around a position, meaning that recruitment and training costs can go down.

While many different aspects of a health insurance plan can benefit an employee, it might not always be accepted by the health care provider. A utilization review is a chance for a health insurance company to look over the different requests of medical treatment that an employee might have given.

Sometimes, a recommended treatment might not be the appropriate one to go through with, so in some cases, a human resource manager might have to work with insurance agents to determine whether or not certain aspects of healthcare are required after all.

Health Care

Utilization review is an audit that consists of the services and costs billed by certain health-care providers.

Self-insurance is an example of a funding feature that might be found in a health plan. Self-insurance is when an employee might decide to not take out any health insurance at all, and rather find a third-party to do so. They might not get any insurance at all, though, with the Affordable Care Act, this isn't supposed to present itself as an option anymore.

Employee Assistance Programs

Employee assistance programs help those that

are experiencing emotional, physical, or other personal problems within a company.

A YMCA membership would not be considered a wellness program. Smoking cessation, child care education, or cancer prevention education could be considered wellness programs depending on company policy.

Those in charge of running a company or certain business might want to include some employee wellness programs to ensure that their staff is healthy and happy. These are programs paid for by the employers and are not things that can be traded for cash or liquified.

For example, an employer might want to hold a cancer prevention meeting in which a professional discusses ways in which employees can prevent themselves from getting cancer. By having educated employees, the employers can be certain that they are doing their best to maintain workers that will live long and remain productive. An onsite fitness center, availability of different types of snacks, or even just having a place where employees can take naps would all be considered a type of employee wellness program.

Employee assistance programs, which might also be referred to as EAPs, are voluntary and work-based programs that offer assessments, counseling, and referrals, usually those that are anonymous. These programs might begin because someone is experiencing work or personal problems.

These programs are paid for by the employers and allow them to make sure that any issues that are affecting their employees can be properly taken care of to ensure that there is no hold-up in the work process.

Chapter 4 – Training and Development

Not only is employee training important, but the development of how that training is going to occur is crucial as well. All of the ways in which employees can learn different knowledge and train in different areas should be well known by a human resource manager that is going to be taking the test.

Finding talent can sometimes be challenging, but that is why it is so important for a human resource manager taking the test to know how to find the right employees that would align with the goals of the company. Training employees can be challenging and different methods for one company might not always be effective for another. It is up to a skilled human resource manager to be able to decipher which training program would work best for a specific organization. In order to do this, different studies should be looked at as well as other methods of training including diagrams and charts.

There are many different training and

development methods that someone could use in a company, but it's important to have a basic idea of all these strategies in order to ensure that they can be easily applied during the taking of the test.

Training and development are both crucial to the roles of a human resource manager, but the two are different from each other. Development refers to the preparation and learning an employee goes through when they have already been working for a business. They might undergo development in order to train for a new position, or just to improve the quality of their work.

Development might include seminars, conventions, or presentations that can increase skill and knowledge. It might be recertification or requiring a higher degree in order to improve the overall knowledge a certain employee has. Training would refer to all of this before, or at the beginning of, the hiring of a new employee.

Training is defined as learning skills that apply to an employee during the current job. Individual learning experiences, preparation of an employee's future career, and the education required to get a certain degree would not be considered training in terms of an HR position.

Training is the process in which an employee learns a particular new set of skills and tools that will be applicable to their time employed with the company. A human resource manager is responsible for setting up an employee's training, but they might not always be the ones in charge of making sure that an employee is trained.

For some companies, a human resource manager will also look at the learning skills that apply to an employee during the current job and figure out whether or not training programs are efficient. A human resource manager will work with those that train others to make sure that the process is going as smoothly as possible so as to make sure the new employee can start regular work as soon as possible, without compromising the learning of any important skills that will help the company improve and grow.

Training is important for obvious reasons, including the necessity to make sure that workers know what they're doing within a certain company. It is also important for a business in an individual sense, as it allows for the business to receive certain benefits as well.

If there is an overall reduction of errors, that means less money is to be wasted and fewer supplies will be used in order to retrain employees or get the risk management involved as it might take time to resolve an issue. There is also less employee turnover. During training, the employee gets the chance to really see what working that position is like, so if they don't like what it involves, they can leave before they become too committed.

It also gives them the chance to get comfortable, so they find it easier to adjust to the certain requirements that a job might include. These are just a few of the benefits of training that should be known by a human resource manager in order to have a high level of knowledge to pass the test.

In 1959, Donald Kirkpatrick created a model that could be used to effectively evaluate the methods of training that a particular company has. By using this model, HRM managers and trainers can look at their training methods objectively to determine whether or not they are effective.

The first criterium in the model is reaction. This takes into account how people might be feeling about a training program and whether or not it is something they are comfortable with. The second criterium is learning. Are people actually learning something from this method of training? The third is behavior.

Are people behaving differently than they did before the training programs? The fourth is results. This might include data analytics that look at the results of a certain training method in order to see if there are actually results coming from what was learned and practiced.

Job analysis is not one of the three phases of training. The three phases of training include planning, implementation, and evaluation. The first phase involves assessing an organization and the training needed to be done. Different employees require different levels of training.

The second step would be implementation, which is the process of training being done. This might include a weeklong training program or one that takes months at a time. The third step would be evaluation, where it is determined whether this training method is effective or not. There are different processes within each of these steps, but they are all individually important to understand on their own level.

Training has benefits that include a reduction in errors and employee turnover. Turnover, in terms of employment, refers to the act of using a new employee as a replacement for the old.

Turnover looks at the number of employees that enter and exit a particular company and the rate at which this happens. Certain positions might have a high turnover, like a fast food restaurant or a retail shop.

Other positions might not have any turnover at all, with the same employees for years at a time. Some positions, like seasonal jobs, might not be affected by turnover as much as others. There are many businesses, however, that might suffer the most from high turnover rates. Recruiting, interviewing, and training all take time and money from a business, so if this has to happen often, profit might not be as high as it could be.

In order to ensure there isn't a problem with the company, a human resource manager should track turnover rates. This can be done with this formula: (Number of terminations) (100) / (average number of employees).

The Learning Process

For some companies, the four phases of learning might differ a bit, but there are certain key elements that can be seen in four different steps. The first involves unconscious competence, which might include a form of preparation. Inciting interest in the company might also be included in this first step.

It might involve a trainer going over what is involved in a day-day operation for a certain business with the new employee. The second stage of learning is coming face to face with these new skills, which is when hands-on training might start. The third would be application and using this new knowledge or set of skills to actually go out there and begin working.

The final stage would be using these skills regularly without any practice. In all of the stages, questioning is the most important in order to ensure that continual knowledge is being taken in by the employee.

A training needs analysis would look at the need for training versus employee training. It would identify if a problem would be fixed by further training, or if that would only make things worse in the end, possibly by spending too much time or money that could be used better elsewhere.

There are different analyses that can be used

that might help someone determine what the results of a training needs analysis would be. These might include other analysis such as individual, task, or organizational.

Those that are in training go through different stages of learning. It might start with just shadowing someone, for example, in a serving setting. They would follow a staff member around as they wait on tables, making sure to keep in mind the duties and responsibilities they're witnessing and using this for a basis of what they're going to do when training has ended.

After that, they might start actually waiting tables themselves, but still with the help of a trained staff member. This would be referred to as active practice. They are actually taking the skills that they have learned in training so far and actively applying them to the job duties that lie ahead.

Behavior modeling is not a strategy used in the behavior modification approach. A human resource manager needs to be aware of different behavior modification approaches in order to determine how to possibly resolve a conflict. Whether this arises during training or during a time an employee is working that has been around a long time, there are different behavior modification approaches that need to be taken in order to remedy various situations. Punishment might need to be taken, but only in forms of reprimand that might include moving someone to a different position or cutting hours. Both negative and positive reinforcement could also help ensure that behavior changes one way or the other.

Job rotation is when trainees are transferred to a different job in the hopes of broadening their focus as well as increasing their knowledge. Within certain companies, different tasks can be done by employees that have the same training.

By moving around positions, employees get the opportunity to broaden their perspectives and look at what different opportunities there might be within a company. Sometimes, if production seems to be lacking or sales are low, a human resource manager might look at what employees could switch positions. By doing this, it might open up new opportunities for both the employees and the company.

Someone in a retail store might be moved from ready-to-wear to jewelry, where they end up performing much better and drive sales even higher. This can benefit the company's sales and the satisfaction of the employee.

Job enlargement is a job design practice that broadens the scope of a job. Job enlargement describes a technique in which there is an increase in the number of tasks that come along with a certain job. Some might assume that a job enlargement would be the process of increasing employees or the amount of work that a company is putting out, but it's about the increase in work that is taken on by an individual. A job enlargement doesn't always necessarily mean a wage enlargement. Sometimes it's necessary for production but other times it might be done to cut down costs or increase overall profit.

Bloom's taxonomy describes the levels of learning in six different steps. The first one is knowledge. This is when previously known information is called upon in order for the advancement of more learning. Comprehension is second, which is when more is understood about what is being learned while applying it to what is already known.

The third is application, in which the first and second step are applied to the new presentation at hand. The fourth level is analysis, in which what is learned and what has yet to be learned is identified. The fifth is synthesis and the sixth is evaluation. It is important for human resource managers to know these six steps in order to ensure that employees are learning in a proper and effective way, whether they're just starting a job or improving on the performance that they already give within a certain position.

KSA

Knowledge, skill, and ability are the words in the acronym KSA. KSA is used often when discussing job duties, evaluations, descriptions, and anything else that might be included overall in a job analysis. The knowledge is what is needed to be known by an employee, either through previous experience or the training that they're going to partake in. Skill involves the set of skills that might be needed by a particular employee in order to ensure that the job is completed. Ability is all about the performance of the employee, whether it's through the expected requirements or through a description of what abilities they might have to possess.

Missions and Goals

A goal is an end and a strategy are how you get there.

Defining purpose as well as laying out the values of an organization could be included in an employer's mission statement. A mission statement is important for any company to have, whether it's been around for a hundred years or is just developing. The mission statement will allow others that don't know much about the business to understand the purpose and direction that the company wishes to go.

A mission statement has three main parts. It will be sure to show the core values that a company holds. What is most important to a company to maintain? The second part would be the goals that a company has. What do they wish to achieve throughout their lifetime?

The third, and most important, is a statement of the objective of the business. A human resource manager should know a company's mission statement inside and out not only to be able to educate new employees but to ensure that the business is also staying in line with their mission statement throughout the ways that they wish to operate.

Operating a program is a cost directly received

by employers. A direct cost is one that can be traced directly to the production of a good or service. An indirect cost is one that is needed to keep the business in operation.

Knowing both of these is important for a human resource manager so they can create budgets and determine different costs of different aspects. It is important to know the difference, so you can price different acts of operational organization needed to make sure that budgets and costs are met.

There are many goals that a human resource manager has, but they are generally individual and organizational. The HRM is responsible for ensuring that an organization reaches its goals, while also making sure that the individual needs of the employees are met as well. The HRM is responsible for making sure that organizational human resources are being fulfilled, while also ensuring that there is an attention to individual employee needs and issues as well. A human resource manager isn't responsible for supervisory goals and instead needs to make sure that they are taking care of individual and organizational goals first and foremost.

Every company needs to make sure that they are setting different goals, both at a corporate and an individual level. These goals might not always be met, but they are important to determine what needs to happen within an organization to meet these particular goals.

This might include doubling profits from the year before, or sometimes even just trying to hire a more diverse set of employees. Before anything else can happen, a goal must be set. Once there is a goal in mind, a strategy needs to be created in order to achieve that goal. A strategy cannot exist without a goal in mind or at least an idea of what one might want to achieve with their specified strategy.

Hawthorne Studies

Hawthorne effect is known as the impact that physical and environmental influence has on employee performance, and in some cases, special notice from a managerial position could help increase motivation in an employee.

The Hawthorne studies is a set of ideas and practices that were studied in Cicero, Illinois at the Hawthorne Works. This study proved that some employees might alter their work if they are aware that they are being watched. The original idea went on to inspire other work-related discoveries, including how a physical and environmental space might affect the employee that's working within that space.

The point of these studies was to focus on the worker's needs, and they did just that, igniting more studies to determine the best way to keep employees happy and efficient. A human resource manager should be aware of the results of the Hawthorne studies as well as other instances of worker's behavior being observed. The more that is known about the scientific reason a worker might act the way they do, the better a human resource manager can think of a solution to help resolve any issues that might arise, whether they're personal or professional.

The Hawthorne study mainly focuses on analyzing and assessing how physical and environmental factors might affect performance. The Hawthorne study puts emphasis on the socio-psychological aspects that might affect human behavior.

This study was conducted within a workplace and helps other employees with information about how their workers might react or handle certain things. The more a human resource manager knows about these important and monumental studies, the better they will be able to evaluate their own employees and ensure that both productivity and performance points are being consistently met at an above average level.

A focus on how an employee's race might affect their position is not related to The Hawthorne studies. The Hawthorne studies aim to look at the impact of physical influence on a company. The physical conditions a job demands will directly affect the way an employee is performing.

If they are in incredibly hot conditions all day, there's a good chance that they might not be the happiest employees. Part of the Hawthorne study also looks at the environmental factors that affect employees. Perhaps the company is located in a very cold area, so foot traffic might not be too high. Low sales could affect employee behavior, so this could be evaluated by the HRM. The Hawthorne study looks more at the things around different workers that can affect their performance rather than the mental socio-psychological factors.

Mentor

A mentor might be given to a new employee in

order to act as an advisor, counselor, or other method of support during the process of training or in the beginning months as they get used to a position.

The mentor would offer advice and feedback on their behavior, as well as give tips to ensure that they find success through this process. A mentor is not to be seen as an authority figure such as someone that would fire, punish, or reprimand the employee. They might suggest behavior modification or present information to a human resource manager should the employee break a serious rule or commit a crime.

Chapter 5 – Employee and Labor Relations

Even though unions might not be as popular as they used to be, knowing all about them and the legalities involved is crucial for anyone wanting to take the test. There is still a very large portion of the test that will cover different union and labor laws.

Proper working conditions need to be maintained, whether it's through the physical layout and safety of a company or through the strategies and methods they use to train and evaluate employees.

There needs to be an understanding of the organizational climate of a company as well as the ability to resolve employee complaints. There are some methods that complaints could be handled, and in a union setting something such as a grievance procedure might be used. Knowing about all of these procedures, programs, and practices is important for those managers taking the test.

Sometimes, a human resource manager might

also be responsible for processing terminations. There are many legalities and regulations that come along with firing someone from their position, and this knowledge will be tested on the exam. It's important to make sure all is known about how to properly let someone go, as well as the different forms of layoffs that might arise in a different company.

A human resource manager needs to understand a culture's organizational features and whether or not this might affect working conditions. There are different theories and practices involved in analyzing a workspace and the overall productivity of that workspace. Any applicant that wants to take the test should have a solid understanding of all of this.

Not only do applicants need to know all of the programs, federal laws, rules, regulations, and acts that affect employers and protects worker's rights, but they also need to be able to apply these. There might be different scenarios presented in which an example is used to express a potential real-life situation. A human resource manager needs to have the ability to asses this different scenario and determine if they know which law applies to which protection. This is important because, in the real world, a human resource manager might have to back up a lower-level employee that is being mistreated by someone that holds a high level of power.

One of the most important aspects that a human resource manager might have to be in charge of is a company's diversity. For too long in American history, there has been a huge lack of diversity in the workforce, with many people passed over because of their race, religion, sex, or gender. As a human resource manager, you will have to be able to identify these different instances of discrimination and understand the proper way to go about resolving the issue so everything is dealt with in a fair and legal way.

Human resource managers should be neutral when it comes to different cultures, backgrounds, and sexes, at least in their working environment. They need to understand what discrimination looks like at its core and how to identify it even when other people might not be aware.

Human resource managers need to be ready and prepared for any kind of discrimination or unfair treatment, and they need to know what to do if faced with a serious issue that could affect the integrity of the business.

A human resource manager that's taking the test needs to be aware of all levels of conflict resolution. This might just involve getting someone their tips they missed out on the previous week, or it could be as big as solving a workplace injury that resulted from two employees fighting. The different levels of severity might be found in the same section, so it is important for human resource managers taking the test to be ready and prepared for any situation.

Those taking the test need to understand the differences among employees in certain workforces and how they interact among others. Different methods of study could come in handy for this section and applying old research methods can help to identify current problems.

HR managers need to be aware of how union and non-union workers are allowed to interact with each other in the workplace, and they need to be cautious of different union recruitment tactics. They also need to understand all the different types of union shops, strikes, and which are illegal, and which are not.

Labor relations might also include performance reviews, promotions, and recognition programs. Sometimes, these all need to be discussed with a manager as well.

This is one of the longest sections on the test, so before getting into more specific details of what should be known, here is a bit more to add to your checklist of things needed to be studied before the test:

- Recordkeeping and the requirements of what should be recorded

- The inclusion of diversity and different awareness programs involved in making transitions smooth among employees of different backgrounds.

- Illness, injury, and prevention when there are different accidents that occur in a workplace. The definition of these injuries as well as what can be done to resolve them is more important information that one needs to understand before going in to take the test.

- All workplace safety and security risks. This will get touched on more in the risk management section, but there are different rules for some aspects of a working environment that should be considered with labor relations as well.

- Emergency response, whether it's to a work-related injury or death, as well as disaster recovery processes and the investigations involved in work-related accidents.

- Business continuity, in terms of who is hired and who is looked pass. There can't be a mistreatment of one protected group and favoritism of another.

- The security surrounding record keeping and the data that has been collected. This can be valuable information for competitors, so it's important to protect all training and operational programs and methods, as well as the personal information of one's employees.

- Collective bargaining and its origin, as well as all terms and concepts associated with a labor union, or other workplace organization that protects a worker's rights.

- The way that performance can be evaluated, as well as how the human resources process can be analyzed as well.

There are three phases that are involved in labor relations. The first one is union organizing. This occurs when workers start to evaluate their own rights and needs, determining if there are steps they need to take in order to increase benefits and decrease inequalities.

The second step would be collective bargaining or negotiation of the agreements of labor. This might include different tactics and strategies to resolve conflict with the employer. The third phase is the administration of contracts, which involves drafting legal agreements with employers to ensure what was discussed is carried out through an agreement.

Collective Bargaining

Collective bargaining is not a phase in labor relations. Recognition, negotiation and administration are all phases in labor relations. Collective bargaining is the act of negotiation with wages or other employee conditions, specifically carried out by an organized group that was typically chosen as others to serve as representation for the thoughts and feelings of the majority.

Collective bargaining might typically be done by the union leaders, or by one representative that was elected by others to be the voice for concern. The Civil Service Reform Act of 1978 protected the rights of workers to organize collective bargaining unions, ensuring that all workers would be allowed to fight for their rights without fear of reprimand.

Unions

The most common types of workers to be in unions are laborers. These might include machinists, auto workers, electrical workers, or other positions of general labor. This is not the limit of the type of job that can be unionized, however. These unions might have their own bargaining unit as well.

A bargaining unit is a selected group of workers that might be the voice of the rest of the workers. They work closely together in a community of shared interests in order to represent the labor union. Knowing the different types of bargaining units and unionized organizations is important, and knowing specific names and titles is helpful as well, both on the test and in a professional setting.

A union organizer that is working within a company that union wants to unionize is referred to as "salting." Salting is the process of a union laborer getting a position of employment with the intention of unionizing that job. A person who does this is referred to as a salt.

This is a legal strategy, even though in some workplace settings, the discussion of unions between members and nonmembers is illegal. If someone is caught salting in a new position, they might be legally fired for not showing genuine interest in a job. Human resource managers should be aware of this tactic to look out for in the hiring process. While not all salters have negative intentions, they might waste training hours and costs if they lie about the time that they plan to spend in a certain position.

Sometimes, an employee might decide that they no longer wish to be represented by their union. If this is the case, they will have to undergo a decertification election. Before that can be done, there must be at least a thirty percent petition for the election, with signatures submitted 60-90 days before a contract is to end. When it comes time for a decertification election, the person that wishes to leave the union will have to receive a majority vote.

Each union creates their own terms and representative resolutions, but there are certain factors that all union officers and human resource managers should know when it comes time for a union election. Once an election occurs, there are many different things that might occur, but before it can even happen, the union workers must show interest. A need for an election must be presented, and at least thirty percent of union workers have to agree to this election for it to take place.

Grievance Procedure

In a union setting, there might be times that disputes arise in which a settlement needs to be reached. In order to resolve conflict, a grievance procedure might be used in order to keep things professional and productive.

The process starts with a written letter to an employer from the union member, in which the grievance would be outlined. This might deal with anything from monetary compensation to personal interactions. The grievance is unique and whatever the employee is experiencing. After that, a meeting will occur in which the grievance will be discussed, and afterward, there will be a settlement.

The point of a grievance procedure is to hopefully come to a resolution in order to fix a conflict that arose. Sometimes, this might mean drafting up a new contract or increasing a certain wage. There are different reasons why a grievance procedure might occur, but many of the steps will be similar once one is decided upon.

If there is no resolution that is met in order to fix a problem, then a third-party determination might come in handy. A third-party determination is when someone else might come in to help find a resolution, and they might even do some speaking or discussing on behalf of one of the members involved in a grievance procedure. Conflict resolution is the purpose of a grievance procedure in a union setting.

Types

A firm that requires employers to pay union

fees if they refuse to join the union is known as an agency shop.

There are many different types of unions that one might experience either in a human resource manager or other employment position. Some unions require membership, others don't. It's important to be aware of all the different types of unions in order to ensure that all the proper rules and regulations are being followed. An agency shop is a union in which an employer could hire union or non-union workers.

Upon employment, that new worker can either join the union or not, based on whatever they would like. If they decide not to join in, they would have to pay a certain fee in order to cover the various collective bargaining.

Members are to become part of the union within a specified time period in a union shop. A union shop might also be referred to as a post-entry closed shop, either on the test or in a professional setting. It is a form of union security in which those that are hired must join a union within a specified period of time.

This enables employees to get a chance to know if they like the position before they decide to commit to that particular union. Every union would create their own specifications for the amount of time that someone has before they make their final decision of whether or not they are going to end up joining the union shop.

Strikes

There are many different strikes that a union might start, and it's important to know the differences between them. An economic strike will happen if a union and employer failed to elicit a new contract that the union wanted in the first place. A union labor practice is one that would come about because the company has asked or been caught up in some illegal behavior or activity. A wildcat strike is one that is unauthorized and usually spontaneous or unplanned. A sympathy strike is one that occurs in support of another strike that is occurring. Knowing all about the different types of strikes is important in order to understand the different rights and agreements that workers and employers have with each other.

A wildcat strike is one that is unapproved by a union. A lockout, secondary, and economic strike are all types of strikes that have been approved by a union before taking place. Before striking, there must be an agreement among the leaders of a union. This is to ensure that this is the proper action to take.

Sometimes, a strike might cause more harm than good, so it's important to make sure that doing one is going to elicit a productive change rather than just be the reaction of some heated emotions. A wildcat strike occurs when there is not any approval from the leading members of a union. A wildcat strike might also be known as an unofficial industrial action.

When a strike has been threatened, it can cause serious tension in the workplace. Most of the time, a strike is the last thing anyone wants to do. Usually, there can be steps taken before a union goes through with a strike. In the chance that it still occurs, a human resource manager needs to be prepared for what to do next. Their main concern is going to be about how service will be maintained as well as any necessary production of the company.

Will services need to be halted, or can another department take on these duties? Of course, the media might get involved, but this shouldn't be the concern of the HRM. There might be money lost and supplies wasted as well, but this would be the concern for someone other than the HRM. It takes an entire union to organize and carry out a strike, so it cannot be blamed on one person either, and if it is, that is in a violation of the very Act that stands in place to protect union workers.

Protective Laws and Acts

As an employee and as an HR manager, it's important for one to know their rights.

Title VII of the Civil Rights Act

Title VII of the Civil Rights Act prohibits employers with 15 or more workers from discriminating, whether it's in an employment, public service, transportation, public accommodations, or telecom position.

Title VII of the Civil Rights Act states:

> "It shall be an unlawful employment practice for an employer ... to discriminate against any individual with respect to his compensation, terms,

conditions, or privileges of employment, because of such individual's race, color, religion, sex, or national origin."

This protects workers from discrimination that are in positions of employment involved in public service or public transportation, and other accommodations or telecom positions. No person can be discriminated against during hiring or firing, compensation, promotion, layoff, recall, recruitment, or pay. A human resource manager needs to be very aware of everything this act protects in order to ensure employees are treated fairly.

Americans with Disabilities Act

Title IV of the Americans with Disabilities Act prohibits mandatory retirement based on an employee's age. The Americans with Disabilities Act is in place to protect anyone that might have a disability. Disabilities include hearing impairments, physical disabilities, and anything else that might give certain workers unfair disadvantages.

In order to ensure these workers don't get discriminated against, the Americans with Disabilities Act covers everything that an employee needs to ensure they will not be discriminated against for any impairments they might experience. This also covers pregnancy, as that will be considered a short-term disability should an employee become pregnant while working for a company.

The Americans with Disabilities Act states that when listing a job description, the most important duty should be listed first in order to give applicants a clear idea of the expectations that might be required of them should they end up in that specific position.

The Labor Management Relations Act

The Labor Management Relations Act protects workers that are in a union from termination and discrimination from their employer based on the fact that they are in a union. The Labor Management Relations Act might also be referred to as the Taft-Hartley Act. It stands to protect workers involved in unions as well as the right of workers to unionize.

It lays out that if workers are not given the opportunity to actively protect their individual and professional rights, then they could cause strikes that might upset the balance of production and commerce.

It also goes on to ensure that employees in a union versus those that are not cannot be discriminated against because of their union status. It is important for human resource managers to be aware of the importance of this act in order to protect union workers rights and be able to easily identify if something wrong is being done.

The Taft-Hartley Act amended the NLRA and addressed unfair labor union practices. The Taft-Hartley Act might also be referred to as the Labor Management Relations Act. This was put in place in order to restrict certain powers that unions have.

It also restricts certain activities and makes it so that laborers have to communicate with their employers about the different activities they plan to involve themselves in. This also requires union leaders to take on a non-communist oath, as well as make closed shops illegal. While unions have many legal rights, employers of different unions do as well, and they need to ensure that unions don't have too much strength to where they can take advantage of their power in numbers.

A human resource manager should know the

differences, power balances, and what's allowed to occur between unions and employers as well as what goes on within unions that might be illegal as well.

Closed shops were made illegal with the Taft-Hartley Act in order to ensure that employers retained a certain amount of power and the activities of unions were limited. In response to the outlaw of closed shops, union shops became popular, which involve employees to have to join a union within a certain amount of time.

This gives employers the chance to pick from a wider pool while also ensuring that union workers have a say over who gets hired as well. Using a union shop versus a closed shop gives a more diverse pool for who might be accepted into the interview process.

Chapter 6 – Risk Management

Safety is one of the most important aspects for a human resource manager to understand. Though there are other departments in place that will help ensure safety standards are being met, it's still up to the human resource manager to oversee all of these aspects in order to make sure they properly carry out different legal procedures.

Risk management used to be referred to as "occupational health, safety, and security." It's essentially the same thing, but now a bit more seems to be covered in the area of "risk." This might include more than just the physical harm of the company.

Risk management is also related to personnel risk. In order to properly pass the test, takers need to be aware of all the forms of personnel risk and how they might be best avoided. Personnel risk might refer to fraud that occurs within a business. They might analyze methods in which employee behavior is tracked, especially when working with finances and voids. They would look to this in order to ensure that there aren't any employees that are taking monetary advantage of a company.

Risk management also includes making sure that all errors are avoided. Sometimes, a simple mistake could really throw an entire business off-track. Someone dealing with risk management would do their absolute best to make sure that there are no errors. They might implement different error-prevention programs and oversee different departments that are in place to make error checks. The methods for doing this should be well known and understood in order to be prepared to go into the test on exam day.

A huge part of risk management is also physical assets. This might include the insurance policies in place to protect different aspects of an office or the production and supply risks that could halt a business's income. Protecting the physical assets of a business environment is crucial in order to maintain that all the employees of a company aren't out of a job should something happen. Disaster prevention methods should be closely studied by those that are going to take the exam. Though some things might not even occur in someone's professional career, they still need to be prepared with this information in order to properly handle whatever might be thrown at them.

HR managers are responsible for ensuring the protection of different technological aspects, which might include installing virus protection programs on the computers of employees. By making sure there is security over all electronic devices, a human resource manager is making sure that all of the company's information is protected, as well as the privacy of the employees. The HR manager might not put these protection agencies in place themselves, but would oversee that they were happening, whether it was through an IT or security department. The methods of taking proper electronic security steps should be well known to anyone going into the test.

Work relationships are also very important in understanding when it comes to risk management. Sometimes, there might be different kinds of lawsuits that a human resource manager would have to deal with. They might have to be the mediator between two employers, or worse, their boss and a lower-level employee. Being aware of all the legal acts that protect workers rights will only help make this process go smoother should a human resource manager ever have to experience this.

Once risk has been assessed, it is also important to understand how to handle it should it happen. This might include filling out the proper forms and checking in with the right department to make sure that everything is being taken care of and smoothed over.

Risk management includes developing systems and implementing programs in order to ensure integrity and safety are maintained and managed among different employees and relationships throughout a company.

When the physical well-being of any person is protected, it is known as safety.

Having little personal control in a job is one of the biggest stress causers in a workplace environment. In order to properly assess what might cause an employee's behavior, it is important to look at everything that might illicit stress or figure out any cause of emotion that could affect their work habits.

One of the biggest causes of stress in a workplace is when an employee feels as though they don't have much personal control. This can cause them to feel as though they are falling behind, and they might not perform as well if they don't have the confidence it takes to know that they can take charge and be confident.

Standards that include general requirements for which machinery is protected in order to ensure it doesn't cause any hazard to employees or the operator is known as machine guarding. The act of guarding a machine, or a training program required by anyone that will come in contact with a hazardous machine within their first thirty days of employment, would have different terms.

Machine guarding involves different rules as well as various physical materials that protect employees from dangerous machines. These standards weren't always in place, but by requiring that certain machines have certain protecting guards, the safety of the employees that are around that machine isn't in jeopardy.

Any machine that might have flying chips, rotating parts, or sparks might require machine guarding. This will usually be very brightly colored in order remind those around that dangerous parts exist underneath.

Falls are the leading cause of death in the workplace. The other three are: electrocution, getting struck by an object and getting caught in-between objects.

The leading place of death of individuals in the workplace are those involved in the construction industry. The Fatal Four is a term coined by OSHA that describes the top four cause of deaths in the construction industry. The first is fatal falling which accounts for over 1-3rd of construction deaths. The following three in the fatal four are electrocution, getting struck by an object, and getting caught in between objects.

Occupational Safety and Health Act

At one point in history, it was cheaper to replace dead or injured workers rather than put safety regulations in place that protected these workers. In order to maintain morality, The Occupational Safety and Health Act passed in 1970 to ensure that companies were doing everything they could to ensure no injury or death occurred that could have been easily prevented.

It is important to remember these years in order to relate them to just how recently workers went without some of these basic rights and protections. It is also important for human resource managers to understand the history of workplace safety in order to prevent it from happening again. While some specific years can be challenging to remember, these precise bits of information are needed to make sure that the test is properly passed.

According to the United States Department of Labor, the Occupational Safety and Health Act exists, "To assure safe and healthful working conditions for working men and women; by authorizing enforcement of the standards developed under the Act; by assisting and encouraging the States in their efforts to assure safe and healthful working conditions; by providing for research, information, education, and training in the field of occupational safety and health; and for other purposes."

1970 is when The Occupational Safety and Health Act passed. The Occupational Safety and Health Administration sets standards for employees in terms of safety and health. They are the administration that is in charge of ensuring employees are taken care of, and if an injury does occur, it is handled properly. There are many different interactions a human resource manager might have with someone from OSHA, so the more aware they are of what is going on within the operations of OSHA, the better they will be able to resolve an issue should one arise.

The dealings with OSHA, such as what forms or procedures need to be dealt with, is important in order to ensure the proper recordings are done. For example, OSHA uses something known as a form 200 to record illnesses, accidents, and injuries. That term alone might be something often discussed within a company and with specific human resource managers and their employees.

Safety Management

Organizational, engineering, and individual are the three approaches to effective safety management. Human resources is not considered one of them and are instead representative of the collective of the three. There are many different procedures a company can choose to use within their safety department and to protect workers. There are some key approaches that should be known by all human resource managers for how different safety management will be effectively used.

One is an organizational approach. What is occurring within an organization that provides safety, and what organizational factors need to be improved upon in order to ensure safety measurements are being reached. Another approach is engineering. Are certain mechanics safe, and are there processes to using machines that are in place to make sure all workers are protected? Another approach is individual. Are the employees safe on an individual level, and can those around an employee feel safe among their fellow workers?

Safety hierarchy refers to the order that actions should be taken in order to eliminate work safety problems. A safety hierarchy can be in reference to the processes of risk control. There are a certain number of actions that need to be taken in order to make sure work safety problems are eliminated.

The first step is to identify anything that might be hazardous or dangerous. A human resource manager has to look around a workplace and the environment that workers will be subjected to and identify each and every hazard that might cause an employee potential harm. The second would be risk identification.

Is there a risk or chance that something might happen? After that, risk assessment and risk control follow to ensure all of these problems are properly dealt with, or that there is at least a plan in place to help if something does happen to go wrong. The final two steps of the hierarchy involve documenting and monitoring the process and continuing the process of keeping everything safe and hazard-free.

Ergonomics

Ergonomics is a work environment design that is the most proper for addressing physical demands that are experienced by people within a business. Ergonomics is the study of how people work efficiently within the environment they are employed. A human resource manager will have extensive knowledge of ergonomics and the practices and studies that come along with the various theories involved with how an employee interacts with their environment.

Ergonomics aims to refine products, tools, and services that help make people's jobs much easier. Ergonomics might involve designing a more efficient desk or computer chair, or it might be more extensive such as developing the method in which a company does the hiring.

MSDS

When a hazardous chemical is processed, stored, or used, an MSDS would be required. An MSDS is a material safety data sheet. These forms are required when there is any handling of a hazardous chemical. Whether this chemical is processed, stored, or used, an MSDS is required in order to make sure that the activity is properly monitored.

They might be placed directly in the workplace, or right where certain hazardous materials are kept and stored. They are reminders to those around that there is hazardous material nearby and certain safety precautions need to be used in order to make sure that no harm can come to the employees involved with it. This also protects employers, as it gives employees the responsibility of properly dealing with these chemicals and materials.

Polygraph Instances

When hiring a guard or member of a security firm that would be responsible for, or have access to, a controlled substance is an instance in which a polygraph test might be administered. Employers are not allowed to give polygraph tests whenever they want, or when an employee calls off sick without a doctor's note. If more than $500 worth of company property goes missing, a police investigation might follow, in which, in rare circumstances, a polygraph test would be administered.

Employers are not allowed to give polygraph tests whenever they want, or when an employee calls off sick without a doctor's note. If more than $500 worth of company property goes missing, a police investigation might follow, in which, in rare circumstances, a polygraph test would be administered.

Most of the time, however, polygraphs are only given when it is important to protect some aspect of security in a job. Whether they are working with classified information or substances that can cause destruction and harm, a polygraph test will likely be administered, but mostly, at the discretion of the HRM or others higher up in the position. Sometimes, if the employee refuses to take a polygraph test, they might not be able to get hired for that position.

Injuries

The overall definition of safety is the condition of protection. When one person can be certain that everything is in place necessary to ensure that they can't get hurt, they will perform much better. It is a natural human instinct to want to feel safe. It is in our biology, so of course, when workers feel like they are safe and protected, they will be able to perform much better than if they were in any other situation.

Accident Investigation

Talking to the person that was injured as well as a witness is very important if an employer wants to conduct an accident investigation and properly fill out the reports. Some companies might exist without ever having to worry about having an accident or causing one of their employee's harm.

Unfortunately, there are plenty of work environments that are prone to accidents, but there are steps to be taken to prevent and resolve workplace accidents. One of the first steps of starting an accident investigation is to isolate the accident scene. The first step is important in making sure that no one else can end up getting hurt in the same way. This is also important to make sure that the scene can't be altered in a situation that might destroy evidence.

The injured worker should be removed immediately, of course, in order to receive proper treatment. The next step is to record any evidence to ensure that it was a complete accident and not something intentional, or something caused by negligence. Recording is also vital in this. After the scene has been assessed, it is time to identify witnesses and speak to the employee that was injured, as long as they are healthy enough and in a state that they can recall what happened.

If an injury or death has occurred, this is considered a recordable case. Some injuries or accidents don't always need to be recorded if they are not very serious. OSHA has certain standards that lay out whether or not an injury is recordable or needs to be recorded.

If it is an injury that cannot be treated with first aid, such as a minor cut, bump, or burn, then it must be recorded. Anytime an employee has to spend days away from work because of the accident or seek professional medical treatment, they need to record their injury.

If there is a loss of consciousness, or even worse, death, this is certainly something that needs to be recorded. If it is an injury that is not work-related, it does not need to be recorded by OSHA.

Drug Use

Disability injuries, injury and illness related deaths, and minor injuries are all defined by the Occupational Safety and Health Act.

Employers can choose who they want to drug test. If drug tests are chosen, they can be conducted in whichever way the employee prefers, including taking blood, urine, or hair samples. Employers don't have to drug test everyone they hire, though they do have to stay consistent with the group they choose to test.

Employers have the right to decide if they want to drug test their candidates or not, but if they choose to do so, they have to ensure that they are being fair with those they pick to test. Only choosing to test a certain candidate is not fair and can be an act of discrimination.

However, only choosing to test employees with more important duties than those with other positions is a common practice. For instance, at a hotel, those that are in high managerial positions might have to be drug tested, but maids or concierge don't have as many responsibilities, so employers might save money by choosing to not test this specific category of workers. In order to ensure there is no discrimination taking place, employers have to make sure they're maintaining consistency with who is being tested.

The Drug-Free Workplace Act

The Drug-Free Workplace Act is in place to inform employees of what might be a violation, spreading awareness, and training supervisors. It does not consider tobacco and alcohol as controlled substances, and it only applies to those employers that have contracts or grants with the government.

One thing a human resource manager might run into often is drug use within the workplace. Some companies might fall under the Drug-Free Workplace Act of 1988, in which a specific grant is received by the company to ensure that they're creating a drug-free work zone. This might involve issuing drug tests and doing extensive background checks on employees to ensure that no drug abuse is taking place.

Those companies that are given grants because of The Drug-Free Workplace Act must inform employees of certain dangers or violations that should occur if drug use is detected. Not all Human resource managers will work for a company that falls under The Drug-Free Workplace Act, but it is still important to be aware of this Act in order to pass the test.

Chapter 7 – Learning and Development

Learning and development is a newer section on the test, so in various study guides and practice quizzes, you might not see this section depending on the year in which the information was written. The basic ideas of this section correlate with the ideas of training and development as well.

Learning and development is all about the contribution to an organizations learning activities. This might include different programs of education to continually teach employees the information they need, or a program that offers assistance in attaining certain degrees or certifications.

This also goes over development, which would include implementation and evaluation of various programs, with an internal consultation and data provider that would help assess the necessity of the programs that have been put in place.

An important part of this section is

understanding the types of consultation and evaluation that can be given to different managers as well as employees that will help them grow professionally, and possibly even personally depending on the company and the morals that are involved. Different developmental activities will also be assessed with employers to determine what can change about a business in order for it to be more productive.

As innovations continue to make life easier for some, they also provide more information to others that can be hard to process. This section is more relevant now as human resource managers have to go over different data analytic methods and look at how they might apply to the learning and development of their company.

A human resource manager will be responsible for contributing succession plans, which would involve the preparation of certain employees for different positions that they are not in just yet. The succession plan would include everything that would be involved in training them and making sure they are prepared to take on their new duties and responsibilities.

Assessing data is important in order to see where costs can be cut, where areas need attention, and what methods of training or development might not have been working thus far. As more tools emerge that can help with assessing data, there's more information that these human resource managers need to learn in order to provide their companies with the most effective knowledge.

Learning and development are both important, but there are also laws and regulations that are in place to protect certain aspects of these as well. Just like all the other sections that will be on the test, it is important to remember the laws put in place to cover or regulate areas of learning and development. This might include the protection of employees and their privacy rights when it comes to collecting data. Human resource managers need to make sure that only fair and legally received information is being used to assess employees and develop their skills further.

Human resource managers also need the tools to develop their own theories about a certain workplace. By taking the theories or studies of other managers, they can apply specific parts to their own company to ensure they are getting proper feedback and the information they need to make correct decisions about what developmental tools need to be implemented within their business.

Some other important aspects of learning and development that human resource managers need to study include:

- Delivery of training programs and facilitation techniques

- Adult learning processes as well as instructional design principles

- The techniques involved to assess different training programs and their efficiency

- Methods of motivation and problem-solving techniques that will aid in organizational development.

- Coaching, mentoring, retention, analysis, task, creativity, and innovative programs and practices that will aid to employee interpersonal growth

This section is all about focusing on individual employees and encouraging their development. It is crucial for human resource managers to look at their employees as people with a lot of knowledge and skill to contribute and not just someone there to perform a task. These innovative thinking processes are results of various studies that should be memorized so they can be applied to situational examples on the exam.

Much like a business lifecycle, a human resource development lifecycle has similar stages. They begin with an introduction, where a human resource manager is aware of their responsibilities, then introducing others to these methods as well.

The second stage is growth, when different aspects of HRM are being smoothed over. The next stage is maturity, when peak management is reached, and instead of dying off like a business cycle, there is a level of management to be maintained with certain standards in place that are concrete and secure.

Determination of availability can be found through the demographic information provided by affirmative action. Affirmative action is a policy that aims to protect certain groups that commonly experience discrimination by ensuring that fair opportunity is given to minorities that might otherwise be overlooked, intentionally or unintentionally.

Sometimes, there might not be as high of a demographic of protected groups in one area as there is another, so there can't be standards set for the number of employees from protected groups that should be hired. Instead, a determination of availability should be explored in order to figure out what percentage of a protected group should be represented within a specific organization.

Chapter 8 – Talent Planning and Acquisition

Talent planning and acquisition is a focus on how different talent is sought out for a position, and what needs to be done to acquire their employment. This involves looking for external sources of employees, or perhaps tracking those with specific skills that might be working in other departments.

What's most important in the acquisition process is following standard laws and regulations that protect current employees as well as those that might end up getting hired. The organizational policies that put legal and ethical requirements in place are important in each chapter, but talent planning and acquisition will especially focus on hiring laws. Some of these important laws include:

- Nepotism

- FLSA

- Independent contractors

- Title VII

- Disparate impact

These ideas might be covered in other sections, but they most apply here to talent seeking. Social media might play a role in this part as well. It won't be a huge part of the exam, but it's important to look into how social media is affecting different acquisition processes of different talent managers. There are still legal standards around using social media in a professional setting, so the test taker should be well-versed in this area as well.

Planning, in all parts of the hiring process, should be very well understood in order to properly identify which steps are right and which other ones might be completely wrong. All parts of a talent acquisition lifecycle should be understood, including the interview process, what happens when an offer is extended, background checks, drug screening, reference checks, and the negotiation process when it comes to terms of employment.

Not only is it important for human resource managers to know where and how to seek out different levels of talent, but they also need to have the abilities to assess talent overall. Are they looking in the right area? Is there a conclusion to be made about the type of applicants? This process of analysis can help better regulate the talent search.

There are likely going to be many questions on types of interviews and the interview process as well. It is important for those taking the exam to be aware of anything they might get asked in relation to interviewing and the legality of what can and cannot be asked. There are many things to include in a job description to keep the company protected from any discrimination, and in each step of acquisition after that, it seems like things only become more regulated.

Acquisition

Checking all references is important when developing hiring plans. Checking references is a way that human resource managers can be sure they are hiring the right employee. There are certain guidelines that need to be considered when checking references, however.

Some companies have rules and regulations that state their employees aren't allowed to give any past information on a particular worker other than their last name and the dates in which they were employed. This protects workers that are no longer in a company from receiving biased feedback that could be false or misinform future potential managers.

Recruiting

Promotion would not be considered external recruiting. External recruiting is any involvement in assessing outside candidates for a certain position rather than looking at the existing staff. This might be done by visiting schools that have future candidates that are about to graduate. Some companies find that hiring those with less experience will require a lower salary.

Using media sources to gauge what is available might also be a form of external recruiting. An employment agency might also be used for external recruiting in order to seek out more qualified candidates that have been carefully selected by different professionals.

Types of Contracts

In some cases, temporary work might need to be hired either to replace an employee that is going to leave, or to make up for the need of a higher workforce, perhaps in busy seasons. In order to protect the company and these temporary workers, a human resource manager might use a third-party contract in order to lay out the terms of the specific agreement between the trust and the company.

The third-party contract would include how much time is expected to be worked and the compensation that will be given for that short period of employment. These contracts might include different terms from what regular consistent employees are receiving as well.

Maintenance

HR managers should locate imbalances among their workforce, so they can remedy the underrepresentation of protected groups with affirmative action.

A citizen of one country that works in a second but is also employed by an organization that is headquartered in a third country is a third country national. It can be hard for those traveling with various visas to keep up with all the rules and regulations, but human resource managers need to be very aware of them all in order to protect the rights of their workers as well as the company from any illegal hiring.

For instance, a human resource manager should be aware of the definition of a third country national, a person that might be applying for a visa in a country that isn't their origin country, but only doing so to go to a different country in order to work. These definitions and restrictions can be confusing for some to remember, so it's important to not just memorize the specifications but also be aware of why they're there in the first place.

Turnover rates can be calculated by taking the number of terminations, times 100, and dividing it by the average number of employees.

The Family and Medical Leave Act

Up to 12 weeks of unpaid leave can be taken during a 12-month period according to The Family and Medical Leave Act, though there are standards that make the time differ depending on the situation.

The Family and Medical Leave Act might be often referred to as or written like FMLA. FMLA protects a worker's rights to take family and medical leave if they need to. They are given 12 weeks within a 12-month period. This might include taking time off for the birth of a child, as well as leave to care for the child, as well as if a child is adopted.

If an employee has a spouse, child, or other close family member with a serious health condition, they might be eligible to take FMLA leave in order to care for them. If the employee themselves has a serious health condition that keeps them from properly performing their job, they would also apply for FLMA. Twenty-six workweeks can also be taken during a 12-month period in order to care for a servicemember that has a serious illness or injury and requires the care of their family member or spouse.

MBO

Measurable goals make up a good MBO. MBO stands for management by objectives, the acronym switched around for obvious reasons. This is a six-step process that is used to integrate managerial activities to improve employee efficiency, as well as achieve corporate goals.

The first step of an MBO is to define organizational goals. This starts with creating goals that are measurable and not ones that are too high to obtain. After that, individual employee objectives should be defined in order to determine what is needed on both a corporate and an individual level. There should be a continual monitoring of progress, with a performance evaluation and feedback to follow. The last step would be a performance appraisal, and the then MBO can start over again.

Conclusion

It is up to the test taker to make sure that they will have all the knowledge necessary to pass the test. You saw in the beginning of each chapter what information is needed to know in order to make sure that preparation has been met. There are plenty of people that don't pass the test, and there is no shame in that. In order to prevent this from happening, spend some time looking at your areas of weakness. If there's a consistent theme among the ideas or questions that you don't understand, try to analyze that to figure out what you need to do to become better prepared.

Perhaps you struggle with different union laws, or maybe remembering dates is challenging. Find a method of studying that works, including flashcards or thinking of a game you can take with classmates or coworkers who are also taking the test. Do whatever you have to in order to make sure that you're understanding the information and not just memorizing it.

Make sure that you find an appropriate place to study. This might mean going to a coffee shop, library, or other place that you can find peace and quiet. Reading in your bed might be fine for certain fiction novels but sometimes studying requires more attention and focus that you won't achieve while snuggled under the covers. Give yourself plenty of time to study before the test and don't try to rush yourself. Even if you think you are prepared to take the test, you might still be lacking information in a section that could give you a low score.

Remember when studying to not completely ignore your strengths or putting emphasis on the knowledge that you're good at. Sometimes, people tend to go over the things they don't understand until they know it better than anything. They might end up neglecting parts they thought they had a decent understanding of, but that might come back to bite them on actual test day. All information needs to be known and understood at the same level.

Do not force yourself to study too much. You might feel the need to study for long hours until the information is understood, but for some people, taking in all this information can be a long process. Though the sooner the better when it comes to certification, it's better to take your time and ensure you know everything needed to pass rather than to try and cram it all in quickly just to get a passing grade. By consuming too much information too quickly, it can all be forgotten just as fast. The best way to actually get to know and understand the information needed is to take it at your own pace, one that includes learning and processing the information.

This is about your future job and status of employment. Though some information can seem tedious or non-applicable, it is all still important knowledge that can help someone not only pass the test but also improve their overall work performance.

Passing the Test

The goal is passing the test. That's why anyone would come to read a study guide. There are some key elements it takes to actually pass a test besides just having an understanding of the information.

A big thing that many people forget to do is to relax. Though the test is timed, rushing yourself will only cause panic. If you don't understand a question, skip it and go back to it later. Some people don't like doing this, but there's a chance that you'll remember the more you get into the test or even a slight chance that the answer exists within another question! Spending 10 minutes just to maybe get one question right is not going to help you pass the test. Instead, spend those ten minutes on questions you know, even if that means completely missing the mark on the one you were originally struggling with. Getting one question wrong is better than not even answering ten different questions.

Preparing for the Test

When the day of the test arrives, it's important to be prepared, relaxed, and focused for the test. Get there as early as possible and make sure to eat breakfast, drink coffee, or do whatever else you might in a normal daily routine. Having a nice meal will help you stay focused during the test without having to worry if your stomach is going to grumble. Trying chewing gum as well, as this can help keep focus.

While practicing this test multiple times can help, it's important that the concepts and ideas are understood rather than just memorized. These are not exact questions of what's going to be on the test, only examples of the information that might be presented. You can also take as many different practice tests as you want but know that you aren't likely going to be able to find any others that contain the current test questions verbatim. Instead, you have to focus on the main concepts that created the questions and figure out how these may be applicable in different scenarios.

It's important to ensure that the study guide has been studied as well and is paired with the practice test in book one. When both are studied, as well as other important information, the test-taker has a much better chance of receiving their certification.

What to Bring

Make sure on exam day that you arrive at least fifteen minutes before your scheduled time. This way, in case something does happen, you'll have already planned to be there a few minutes early so your time won't be as late had you expected to get there right on time. If you arrive too late, you risk losing your chance to take the test without getting a refund on any fees paid.

Bring your ID; the type doesn't matter as long as it's not expired, and it's government issued. This might include your passport or driver's license. If you do not bring this with you, you will not be able to receive your test or certification, no matter how knowledgeable and prepared for the information you might be. It's important to not forget small things like this in order to ensure that nothing gets in the way of you getting your certificate!

Good luck!

CPSIA information can be obtained
at www.ICGtesting.com
Printed in the USA
BVHW090911290621
610723BV00004B/1306

9 781617 045196